Canadian Corporate Directors
on the
Firing Line

Canadian Corporate Directors

on the
Firing Line

Murray G. Ross

McGraw-Hill Ryerson Limited

Toronto   Montreal   New York   St. Louis   San Francisco
Auckland   Bogotá   Guatemala   Hamburg   Johannesburg
Lisbon   London   Madrid   Mexico   New Delhi   Panama
Paris   San Juan   São Paulo   Singapore   Sydney   Tokyo

Canadian Corporate Directors on the Firing Line

ISBN 0-07-092422-8

1 2 3 4 5 6 7 8 9 10 D 9 8 7 6 5 4 3 2 1 0

Printed and bound in Canada

Canadian Cataloguing in Publication Data

Ross, Murray G.
  Canadian corporate directors.

Bibliography: p.
Includes index.

ISBN 0-07-092422-8

1. Directors of corporations—Canada.
2. Corporation law—Canada.   I. Title.

KE1402.R67   346.71'0664   C80-094485-2

To

The First Board of Governors of York University (1960-65)

Of all the boards on which I have served, this was
the finest in terms of competence, dedication, sense
of purpose and duty.
M.G.R.

CONTENTS

Preface

It will be some years hence before the definitive book on corporate boards appears in print. The reason is that very little research has been done on this important segment of corporate life. This is the more surprising since faculties of administrative studies have proliferated in universities in the past decade. But their research has been largely concentrated on management and little, if any, attention has been given to the governance of corporations.

Why then a book on the boardroom now? There are a number of reasons: first, attitudes about boardroom practices are changing—rapidly in society, more slowly among directors; secondly, the law, ambiguous about and protective of directors as it may be, promises to be far more severe and demanding than it has been in the past; and, finally, lessons have been learned through experience, experimentation is taking place and then being studied and recorded, and a boardroom literature is being developed. For all these reasons it is important to draw upon such trends and wisdom as are available, to present a clear and current picture of the issues and problems that surround corporate directors. Such an exercise should be repeated regularly.

The literature on corporate boards that is now available is largely fragmented. There are papers and occasional books by lawyers on the legal interpretations of liability and indemnity; studies by bodies, such as the Conference Board, on attitudes, practices, composition, compensation, etc., of existing boards; detailed analyses of certain board responsibilities, such as the audit committee, by firms of accountants; etc. The most significant of the above is written by legal experts who advise boards. My own experience is that many board members, relatively confident of their own comprehension of their duties and the information and counsel they receive from management, auditors, and solicitors, bother very little with any of these publications. Most board literature is presumably written by experts and is aimed at specialists.

This book was written by a lay person for lay people. It is not a technical book; it seeks to present in readable form the issues facing corporate boards at the present time, to outline what appear to be the responsibilities of directors in this new era, and to propose reforms that will bring current practice into line with public expectations.

In preparation for writing I examined a broad range of material written by lawyers, auditors, directors (both lay and professional), as well as accounts of corporate and directorate activity in books, journals, and newspapers. Along with this I have drawn on some forty years of experience on committees and boards of both profit and non-profit corporations. I am certain I have served on some of the worst as well as some of the best boards in Canada and have, I hope, learned from both. The result is therefore a product of research, study, and experience—all, of course, conditioned by subjective judgment. Another person with the same experience might have examined the same materials, but written quite a different kind of book.

Inevitably, I have had to devote a good deal of time to acquiring some knowledge of the law as it applies to directors, their terms of reference, their duties. It need hardly be said that this was an onerous task for one not trained in law. Legal documents do not lend themselves to easy reading for the lay person, and to translate legal doctrine into a form and language that would be comprehensible to others was a formidable undertaking, the success of which only the reader can judge. Yet my involvement in law was not without its rewards, for the law is the beginning—the basis—for consideration of directors' duties. Whatever else directors must do, they must obey the law. Thus, some understanding of what government Acts, regulations, and the courts say about directors and their responsibilities is an essential beginning for the conscientious director.

I cannot claim that what I have written about the law and its implications for directors can be read without annoyance. Many legal documents defy precise translation and must be quoted directly. But I have attempted to be selective in quoting and to provide only enough information to alert directors to certain key passages without a knowledge of which they would be unprepared for their duties as directors. One legal friend, who tends to be somewhat intolerant of lay people who "dabble in the law," after reading the relevant legal passages in my manuscript commented, "It is unsophisticated law but not inaccurate!" This judgment is satisfactory to me. If what I have written is accurate and understandable I will feel rewarded for the hours spent reading extremely dull and unnecessarily complex (to my mind) legal material.

Though some corporate lawyers seem loath to mention it, the law merely outlines the minimum requirements for directors. The 1970s saw many changes in boardroom practices in both profit and non-profit corporations in the United States and the recent literature on directors in that country presses for even further improvements and reforms. Sophisticated directors today, in both Canada and the United States, are aware of much broader ethical and social responsibilities than is found in the law, both with respect to internal corporate behaviour and to a host of external (community) issues which are affected by corporate decisions. Thus my proposals for directors' duties and board reform go well beyond anything required by law.

I was led also to a consideration of the structure of Canadian profit corporations, with what was for me some surprising results. Chapter 7 reports on the result of this investigation, which illustrates the very considerable difficulties directors of most Canadian profit corporations face if they attempt to carry out the duties that both the law and the public expect them to perform.

With the exception of the chapter on shareholders and directors in profit companies (Chapter 7), most of what is said in this book applies to both profit and non-profit corporations. There are, of course, important differences in these types of corporations to which I make several references, but as far as boards are concerned the responsibilities of directors are very similar, both in law and in public expectation. As many directors serve on boards of both profit and non-profit corporations, an interesting study would be how these directors conceive their roles in these two different types of corporations. I tend to believe their attitude and behaviour differ between the profit and non-profit corporation, but in fact it should be much the same, for in both the director has very similar legal and moral responsibilities. Thus, I hope that directors in both types of corporations will ponder the questions and guidelines presented in this book.

I am most grateful to Messrs. Floyd Chalmers, Malim Harding, and Lionel Goffart for reading and commenting on my manuscript. Each provided valuable suggestions which I have incorporated in my final draft, but no one other than myself is responsible for the content of this book. Mrs. Carol Pratap kept my expanding files of material in good order during my period of research and typed the manuscript in draft and final form. I am most appreciative of her conscientious and skilful work.

Murray G. Ross
Toronto
January, 1980

A Director: To Be or Not To Be

I

Robert Benchley is reported to have divided people into two categories: those who divide people into categories and those who don't.

It is only a slight exaggeration to suggest that attitudes toward directors of corporations may be divided into two categories: positive and negative. The negative attitudes dominate in our society and have infiltrated even the boardroom itself, although in a much less vocal manner.

There are many who see boards of directors as anachronisms—part of an institutional structure whose days of usefulness have passed. The most common concern is that most boards are merely "a rubber stamp" for the chief executive officer of a company, university, or hospital. Frequent criticisms are that directors are appointed to give status to the organization, accept few responsibilities, and take their duties with something less than devotion.

This, of course, is a serious accusation but there is some justification for it. Some years ago Myles Mace of Harvard School of Business did a study of directors of widely held manufacturing, mining, and retail companies, and concluded that there was a considerable difference between what directors were supposed to do and what they actually did. Few directors conceived of their jobs as directors as being onerous, time-consuming, or difficult.[1] "The title and prestige of candidates are regarded as of primary importance in the selection process as well as their reputations as noncontroversial and sympathetic understanders of the system; boat rockers are not usually the choice of presidents—the top executives of corporations, academic officials, and leading partners of financial institutions and law firms—are extremely busy people who can devote limited amounts of time to serving as directors of other companies."[2] These directors are some-

---

[1] Myles Mace, *Directors: Myth and Reality* (Boston: Harvard University Graduate School of Business Administration, 1971).

[2] Ibid, pp. 106-107.

1

times seen, as Mace puts it, as "attractive ornaments on the corporate Christmas tree."

There have been changes, since the Mace study, toward greater director responsibility, but a recent study by Peterson for the Conference Board in Canada suggests that while some directors are conscious of the need for greater activity and accountability on the part of their boards, very few boards have yet made this adjustment.[3] While it has sometimes been suggested that trustees and governors of hospitals, universities, and other non-profit agencies give more time and effort to these institutions, there are no data to support this view, and it is not difficult to identify many such trustees, directors, governors, etc., who sit on the board merely for the prestige and/or companionship such membership provides. Almost all non-profit boards carry some "deadwood."

Thus there is some support for the criticism of those boards that are confined to a small genial elite, give little time to the direction and operation of the corporation, and conceive of their responsibilities as occasionally offering advice and support to management. The expectation that they should form a critical part of the corporate structure and therefore share in the leadership and direction of the corporation is rejected, at least in practice, by many directors.

While the above criticisms seem to have penetrated the boardroom enough to encourage a hope for change, there are other more cogent arguments that the modern board must face. One of these is to challenge the legitimacy of the board. Those who raise this issue assume the board has considerable power in the direction of the corporation (as, of course, it should have) and the question relates to the use or abuse of this power. What right have you, these dissenters ask, to sit on a board which makes decisions that affect the lives of hundreds of workers and customers? What qualifies you to be a director and to make such decisions? What justification is there for *you* to serve on the boards rather than hundreds of other equally, or more, able people? What assurance is there that you give adequate attention to the public interests and not simply to a very narrow objective? These, of course, are the questions that swept university campuses in the 1960s and they are still very much alive, not only among academics but among many groups on the political left in Canada.

Before dismissing these questions as simply the raving of a few radicals, one needs to recall the appointment of workers to corporate boards in Sweden and Germany; the move by the European Eco-

---

[3] Susan Peterson, *Canadian Directorship Practices: A Critical Self-Examination* (Ottawa: The Conference Board in Canada, 1977).

nomic Community to make worker representation on company boards compulsory; the Bullock Report in Britain which is sympathetic to more representative company boards than existed in the past; and the agreement that permits the United Automobile Workers to place a representative of the Union on the Board of Chrysler Corporation.[4] One may also recall that University of Toronto abolished its Board in 1969 and gave power to a Governing Council made up of students, faculty, alumni, and a number of government appointees. None of these changes may spread to Canadian corporations but it would be a mistake not to realize that there is a considerable body of opinion that questions the competence of many board members and the way Canadian corporate boards operate.

What has replaced the radicalism of the 1960s is a new consciousness of the total environment in which we live and a desire, if not a demand, that everyone have a share in determining the shape of the future. Ralph Nader perhaps led the way with the manner in which he challenged institutions which seemed to be accountable only to themselves. In his auto safety campaign he not only stood up to some of America's most powerful corporations but won a good deal of public support for his position. More recently Jane Fonda and her husband, Tom Hayden, have been leading another reform movement: "People feel shut out of the economic decision making process and the only way they are going to be allowed in is through representation on the boards of the structures that are the real power centres of the country."[5]

Perhaps more important than these developments is what is identified as the new "Middle Class Activism"[6] of the late 1970s. "What has happened, it seems, is that the powerful institutions on which the middle-class could rely are no longer reliable, no longer accountable. They serve other interests as well. Business serves itself in ways that even the middle-class find offensive."[7] The middle class, it is claimed, represents a new reform movement: "By the standards of the 1960s they are unrecognizable as protesters, their dress is neat, their tone moderate, their battlegrounds indoors, not out. Their goals are equally remote from the Sixties. Instead of peace, civil rights, and an end to poverty the goals are consumer protection, auto and air-

---

[4]"UAW is dead serious about place on boards," *The Globe and Mail,* 13 August 1979, p. B6, and *Time,* 5 November 1979, p. 64.

[5]*The Globe and Mail,* 7 October 1979, p. 9

[6]*Saturday Review,* 8 March 1975, pp. 12, 14, 15.

[7]Ibid, p. 13.

plane safety, limited growth, pure food, clean air and water, cleaner politics, and especially 'accountability.'[8]

Of all citizens, corporate board members are perhaps the least sensitive to such stirrings in society. There appears to be something in the boardroom that immunizes them from recognition of a potential threat to their position. Take for example the heavy fine in 1979 leveled against Joseph E. Seagram and Sons for illegal activity. ". . . the liquor company pleaded guilty to bribery charges linked to illegal political contributions and sales promotions payments . . . Seagram, also accused of illegally funneling thousands of dollars in bribe money from the parent company in Montreal to its American headquarters in New York City, agreed to pay all fines and penalties."[9]

A study of the reaction of corporate executives and a sample of citizens to Seagram's activities would be revealing. It is, of course, pure speculation to suggest that board members would say "Seagram's is an exception" or "they are in that kind of business," whereas a sample of citizens would probably ask "don't all big companies act this way?"[10] There is not an adequate recognition in the boardroom of public attitudes, expectations and possible actions. The prevailing view of business is underlined by one commentator: "Considering today's corporate view of society and the most outrageous forms of misbehaviour that result, it is clear the seeds of potential business decline lie not with some outside socialist menace but within business itself."[11]

There is another question about the effectiveness of the corporate board which arises from the greatly expanded role of government in the affairs of all citizens. The extent, scope, and cost of government regulations which impinge on individual corporations is immense but await careful research to reveal all the implications for both society and the corporation. One amusing but revealing report on the U.S. Labor Department's Health and Safety Administration indicated thousands of rules dealing with such minutia as the shape of the toilet

---

[8] Ibid, p. 12.

[9] *New York Times*, 31 September 1979, p. E5.

[10] *York Gazette*, Vol. 10, no. 10, p. 3. (A report of a survey of student opinion in Ontario universities in 1979.) "Even more striking is the fact that 89 per cent hold a negative view of business in general . . ."

[11] J. Richard Finlay, "Are Canadian Firms Putting Profits Before Responsibility? *The Toronto Star*, 21 April 1979.

seats, the proper height from the floor at which fire extinguishers must be hung, and hundreds of other "Mickey Mouse rules."[12]

Such regulations may or may not have validity but their number is overwhelming. More important is government intervention in fundamental policy decisions. Professor Isaiah A. Litvak in an article on "The Ottawa Syndrome" indicates "The government is an active partner in the management of business as it both influences and controls more and more of the basic management decisions of the firm, ranging from choosing new products and processes to setting prices and determining which production methods to use."[13] James Thackray, President of Bell Canada, indicated that the Department of Corporate Affairs through the director of investigation and research has continued to harass Bell and Northern for more than twelve years in trying to break them up,[14] and "Imperial Oil Chairman, Bill Twaits, drew cheers in the spring of 1977 when he told a corporate seminar that the private sector had been kicked around by legislation, regulation and downright abuse."[15]

In non-profit agencies, many of which have all or parts of their budget provided by government, the latter, inevitably, tends to develop rules and regulations that are tantamount to determining policy. In 1979 the Ontario Hospital Association issued a guidebook to hospital trustees in which it said: "The Government is, increasingly, attempting to direct how health care resources should be allocated within individual communities. . . . We accept budget restraints . . . that may be necessary in the current situation. The government must attempt to achieve this objective, however, with cooperation and assistance of community trustees and physicians and *not by arbitrarily assuming the trustees' role*"[16] (italics mine). In universities as well, many people feel the government dictates policy and often deals directly with the university administration, thus by-passing the university's board of governors who are charged with the responsibility for the welfare of the university.

All this is relevant to the question at hand. There are those who

---

[12]*New York Times,* 26 November 1978, p. 4E.

[13]*The Business Quarterly* (London: University of Western Ontario), Summer 1979, p. 23

[14]James C. Thackray, "Regulation, Profit, and the Public Interest" (Speech given at 67th Annual Meeting of Ontario Chamber of Commerce, Ottawa, May 8, 1979).

[15]Reported in *Toronto Star,* 20 March 1979, p. A10.

[16]*Hospital Trustees as Governors and Managers* (Don Mills: Ontario Hospital Association, 1979), p. 3.

think that the role of government has expanded so rapidly, and the regulations in respect of corporate behaviour have changed so frequently, that the responsibilities of directors have become not only ambiguous but in some situations non-existent. The line of contact seems increasingly to be one between management and various government agencies. In day-to-day relationships between government and corporate officers, the board is often overlooked.

There is another quite different reason why some people are concerned about the future of corporate boards; this being the new interpretations of the legal obligations of directors. It may seem incongruous that as the complexity of government regulations makes the role of directors less meaningful, some regulations call for directors to be far more diligent, prudent, and competent than in the past. Legally, the directors are responsible for the management of the corporation. Hitherto this responsibility may have been taken lightly, but in recent years the number of class-action, shareholder, and government agencies' suits against corporations in the United States has increased enormously. There have been relatively fewer such actions in Canada, but this is now beginning to change as we will see in Chapter 5.

If one is to serve on a board faithfully, one is required to give far more time to this task than the two hours a month that was the practice in the past. One Canadian who is a director of a large U.S. corporation reported that he spends four full days a year as a member of the Audit Committee, in addition to regular meetings of the board. "Any new member coming onto the board of a large corporation today faces a workload unimagined a decade ago. Texas Instruments, for example, now requires a minimum commitment of thirty days per year by an outside director."[17] If one is already deeply committed to one's own job, such amounts of time could be an intolerable burden. Even if a board member serves conscientiously, he still cannot be certain of not facing a lawsuit at some time for reasons often beyond his control. One director who served on a board of a U.S. corporation which, after long deliberation, rejected a take-over bid was faced with legal action by a group of stockholders who thought the board acted irresponsibly. But, as he said, if the board had decided that the take-over bid was fair and agreed to it, members of the board would be sued by another group of shareholders who were convinced that the take-over offer was inadequate. It was a no-win situation! It is in light of these difficulties that a lead article in the *New York Times* asked, redundantly, "Who Will Serve on Tomorrow's Boards?"[18]

---

[17]*New York Times*, 25 February 1979, p. F3.

[18]Ibid.

The total effect of this skepticism and questioning about the role of boards of both profit and non-profit corporations is to raise in the minds of directors and non-directors the problem of the structure of modern corporations. Are boards an essential part of this structure? If so, what should be their precise responsibilities? In light of changing social circumstances can corporate directors possibly meet both the legal requirements and public expectations of their responsibilities? We will return to these questions in later chapters. At this point we need only say that one cannot assume that boards of directors, trustees, governors, etc., will continue to exist without substantial changes to reverse the many negative attitudes toward them which presently exist in Canada.

II

There is, on the other hand, strong support for the present organization of the corporation which involves a board in making and/or approving major corporate decisions. Scrutiny by such a group is likely to be on the basis of a broader perspective and with wider concerns than that of management. Many who have served on boards of both profit and non-profit corporations have made major contributions, in terms of knowledge, experience, and insight, to the welfare of corporations. Many boards have worked well, and as the criticism and doubts spread, the efforts of more boards will likely improve.

Boards, of course, operate at varying levels of efficiency and effectiveness. At the very least a board acts as a kind of disciplinary force in the corporation. Management may be free to operate, doctors to practise in hospitals, professors to teach, but all are conscious of the existence of a board—a higher authority—which, however inadequate, has the right and responsibility to enquire about their activities. A group of doctors in a hospital formed a private profit-making pharmaceutical company to which some doctors in the hospital referred patients with drug prescriptions. When this was discovered by the hospital board, the doctors were given the choice of staying with the hospital and dissolving their drug company or leaving to run their private practices and business. Needless to say, this obvious conflict-of-interest may well have continued if a board had not existed. The very fact of a board's existence, however inept it may be, may well deter management from engaging in questionable practices. Even the weakest board serves this function; the best boards perform in a manner which creates a sense of responsibility for high standards that pervades the whole corporation.

Myles Mace, in his study of corporate boards, found many inadequacies in practice, but in his summary he states: "Almost all the executives interviewed stated that the concept of accountability to a board, even a board composed of the most understanding and sympathetic friends, provided an important discipline for the organization—'especially for the vice-presidents'—as one executive stated. The feeling of accountability to a legally constituted body such as the board of directors resulted in a closer examination and analysis of results, a more faithful fulfillment of what was called 'corporate homework,' and an increased interest in avoiding careless and ill-prepared presentations to the board. Boards of directors do provide some sort of discipline for business corporations—a sort of corporate conscience."[19]

Further, boards are usually composed of people who are experienced in the affairs of the community and/or of business. All this experience is of unquestionable value to a chief executive officer (hereafter CEO) if he is wise enough to call upon and follow any useful advice. As one CEO said, the board provides "additional windows to the outside world."

The traditional role of the board has been one of advising, disciplining, and decision making in crisis situations such as hiring or changing the CEO. These functions are not sufficient to justify the existence of a board in light of the new demands made on corporations by the law, consumer and church groups, security commissions, and shareholders or members.

There has been, as several studies suggest,[20] a growing awareness in Canada of the expanding responsibilities of boards, which is likely to be a prelude to widespread changes in board practice. The Southam Company has quarterly board meetings, two of which are full-day sessions and two of which are two-day sessions which often carry over for another half day. And, as the Peterson study[21] shows, there is a gradual acceptance of the need for intensive committee and board work in the modern corporation. The responsibilities outlined in Chapters 5 and 6 may soon be accepted practice in the modern profit or non-profit corporation, making the board a vital and necessary part of the organization.

---

[19]Mace, *op cit*, p. 4.

[20]Peterson, *op. cit.*

[21]Ibid.

III

In spite of criticisms and doubts, boards of directors (or trustees or governors) will continue to exist, if only because a corporation is required by law to have such a board. However, board members must be made to respond to justifiable criticism with positive action. A good deal of the criticism is most certainly uninformed; for example, the corporate structure cannot be an absolute political democracy and survive. Further, much criticism is often simply an effort to find a "scapegoat," to alleviate the problem of trying to understand very complex issues. In 1979 some curators of the Royal Ontario Museum attacked the board and its directors on the grounds of "mismanagement"—a simple phrase which hardly took into account a very difficult expansion program, a year of government financial restraints, and a board of highly responsible men and women with broad experience and financial skill. Although many attacks on boards are made with little understanding of all the facts, this does not absolve directors, for there are still many reforms crying for implementation.

Directors must face a new reality: "Changes in laws and regulations and mounting social, consumer, and employee pressures are changing any lasting flicker of the honorary nature of a directorship to one demanding substantive performance and public accountability. No longer can a board be confined to an exclusive group of friends selected by the CEO or chairman. No more can a director merely direct (if he ever did), nor can he just merely reflect. Questions of whether the director is an advocate or an advisor, tiger or lamb, figurehead or a keeper of a fiduciary trust, are welling up in boardrooms. This provokes rethinking the philosophy, concept, structure, composition, role, and effectiveness of the board and the fit of individual directors."[22]

---

[22]Robert K. Mueller, *New Directions for Directors* (Lexington, Mass: Lexington Books, 1978).

The Various Corporations and Their Purposes

I

When one speaks of corporations today the tendency is to think of large business corporations—to judge by the media most are "multinational corporations." While it is true that these are the largest and most powerful of modern organizations, they represent, even with their subsidiaries, only a proportion of legally constituted corporations in Canada. There are hundreds of small independent companies, thousands of non-profit corporations and many other types, all legally registered as corporations.

Before commenting on the philosophy which led to the requirement that corporations have boards of directors, it may be useful to review the variety of corporations which exist and the differences in their purpose and nature.

The word "corporation" is close to being a generic term and means simply a form of organization which is given legal status in our society. Chief Justice Marshall defined a corporation as "an artificial being, invisible, intangible, and existing only in the contemplation of law." Another great jurist, Justice Denning, said: "[A corporation] may in many ways be likened to a human body. It has a brain, a nerve centre which controls what it does. It also has hands that hold tools and acts in accordance with directions from the centre. Some of the people [in the corporation] are mere servants and agents who are nothing more than hands to do the work and cannot be said to represent the mind and will. Others are directors and managers who represent the directing mind and will of the company and control what it does. The state of mind of these managers is the state of mind of the company and is treated in law as such. So you find—in law—the fault of the manager will be the personal fault of the company."[1]

However useful such definitions may be to the legal profession, they describe inadequately the reality of what the corporation is. A non-legal pragmatic definition might be that *the corporation is a collective organization with a legal and constructive purpose, which engages a per-*

---

[1] Vincent Powell-Smith, *The Law and Practice Relating to Company Directors* (London: Butterworths, 1969), pp. 78-79.

son(s) to develop means of achieving this purpose and has a responsibility to its shareholders or members and to the public to make serious and honest efforts to fulfill the purposes it has established for itself.[2] This, of course, neglects the fact that an individual (as opposed to a group) may be incorporated and also, by inference, that many consider incorporation to be a right that can be withheld only in very exceptional circumstances. But the profit and non-profit corporations with which we deal in this book are collectives, that is, groups of individuals who seek to achieve some goal that has been established for the corporation. Some would argue that such corporations do not have any responsibility to the public and legally this is probably the case. But increasingly one hears the phrase "a good corporate citizen" and most leader-corporations now accept the fact that "the public interest" is a matter to which attention must be given when major decisions are to be made. However one may regard the decision of Sun Life to move its head offices from Montreal to Toronto, one would agree that this decision would have been made far more readily had the officers and directors of Sun Life not been aware of their public responsibilities and of the consequences in Canadian life of the decision they were asked to make. Therefore, while the definition suggested above may not have legal validity, it appears to be a sensible and realistic description of the modern corporation we deal with herein.

Why do individuals and groups incorporate? It varies with the type of corporation and the following reasons do not apply to all organizations. Generally incorporation provides for limited liability to individual members of the corporation; it provides the right to issue shares, raise capital, borrow money; it provides for continuity of operation (an individual who operates an unincorporated business may die and his business with him); it means shared risks; it permits, in some cases, tax exemptions, in others, tax concessions; and in this day of holding companies and conglomerates it provides what is, in effect, tax shelters for some corporations and some individuals.

Incorporation is by far the most popular form of organization in our society for many different endeavours.

II

For our purposes there are two major types of corporations: profit and non-profit corporations.

The purpose of a profit corporation is, of course, to make a profit.

---

[2]This definition is not consistent with the law, which does not require the corporation to set out its objectives.

This is not meant to be a pejorative statement; to the contrary, it is the excess of income over expenditures which provides the capital to replace outworn equipment and to reinvest in new machinery and technology. This is not to say that the profit corporation does not have other responsibilities, as we will suggest in later chapters, but if the objective of making a profit is not consistently sought, the forces of the market will cause it to fail.

There are many kinds of profit corporations, some of which, such as banks and insurance companies, operate under special legal requirements. Their boards of directors must be well informed about these unique regulations, as well as fulfilling those obligations common to other boards.

Another variation is the one-person or one-family corporation with no outside directors, direction, or control. The company is privately owned and operated. (Such corporations may, of course, have a board of directors, but if the company is a small one the board would probably be composed of an individual director or one of two of his family, friends, or employees.) It may have only one director who may also be the CEO.

There are many other types of profit corporations, some widely held with many shareholders, some with many shareholders but with an individual, group, or company holding sufficient shares to control the corporation, as well as the one-shareholder corporation, usually a completely owned subsidiary of a parent company.

There is another category of corporation which falls somewhere between traditional conceptions of profit and non-profit corporations. These are the multitude of Crown corporations, many profit orientated, but some service and often subsidized corporations. The precise number of federal corporations[3] and their provincial counterparts appears to be somewhat obscure but "according to the latest tabulations federal Crown corporations had . . . total assets of nearly $28 billion while their provincial cousins held assets worth another $39 billion."[4] These corporations, such as Air Canada, the Cape Breton Development Corporation, the Canadian Broadcasting Corporation; the National Film Board, etc., constitute a major financial and cultural force in Canadian life.

These corporations are established by special statute (for example, the St. Lawrence Seaway Authority Act) by letters patents, or by ar-

---

[3] *The Royal Commission on Financial Management and Accountability* (Ottawa: Ministry of Supply and Services, 1979), p. 328.

[4] David Perry, "A Taxpayer's Guide to the Business of Government," *Financial Post 300*, Summer 1978, p. 47.

ticles of incorporations under the Canada Business Corporations Act. Each has its own board of directors whose responsibilities should include those outlined in Chapters 5 and 6. There are, however, some difficulties here: the boards are usually appointed by government, and while they do maintain a degree of freedom they are required to report to a minister who can, and often does, influence the direction and management of the corporation. Further, these corporations are subject to government policy and to changes in this policy. The role of the director in such a corporation, if he is at all diligent and honest, is often a difficult, if not hazardous one.

While directors of non-profit corporations bear most of the same legal responsibilities as those of profit corporations, the nature of the two institutions is quite different and requires some elaboration. There are literally thousands of non-profit corporations in Canada ranging from hospitals with $100 million annual budgets to small local art galleries with budgets of only a few thousand dollars. Most non-profit organizations are formed to provide a service; unlike profit corporations their criterion of success is not "the bottom line" of profit or loss but the quantity and quality of service they offer. Directors of these corporations are thus called upon to make highly subjective judgments about these services, often without hard data to justify their decisions. In many cases they receive some guidance from professional staff members, but their obligation is to manage the corporation and not to be managed by the staff.

There are major differences among these non-profit corporations about which directors should be aware. Etzioni[5] distinguishes three types of organization: (a) coercive (such as prisons, where coercion is the necessary force to secure action); (b) remunerative (such as business, in which various kinds of material benefits are the prime motivating force); and (c) normative (such as churches, political parties, universities, in which dedication or allegiance to the purposes of the organization is a major factor in keeping the organization together and functioning well). These, of course, are broad categories, which do overlap. Nonetheless it is important to recognize that in the normative organization (which would include most non-profit corporations) motivation among those in the organization is nourished less by force or remuneration than by dedication to the service offered. This makes for quite a different atmosphere in the organization as the purposes of the corporation must be constantly visible and its achievements consistently related to these ends. Thus, one tends to

---

[5] Amitai Etzioni, *A Comparative Analysis of Complex Organizations* (New York: The Free Press, 1971).

find in these organizations long discussions of "matters of principle" and while some find such discussions tiresome, it is important to remember that these often serve to clarify and reinforce the purposes of the non-profit corporation. The members of such organizations tend to be "democratically oriented" and likely to be intolerant of authoritarian leadership and much more amenable to discussion and consensus in dealing with even minor operational problems. (Thus the great disputes that take place in hospitals and universities about what staff members consider to be "arbitrarily imposed parking fees.")

Directors of charitable non-profit corporations are not permitted financial compensation but they have the same responsibilities in respect of conflict of interest and financial management as directors of profit corporations. Indeed the responsibility in respect of the latter may be greater since the staff of non-profit corporations is seldom chosen for its ability in financial management and one of the major contributions of the board is to develop financial strategy and achieve a degree of financial control.

It should be noted also that many of these non-profit corporations, such as hospitals and universities, operate under special provincial Acts, and while there are only slight variations in them every board member should be aware of the conditions set forth in the relevant Act.

Directors of non-profit corporations seem to be more subject to public criticism than their fellow directors in profit corporations. The non-profit corporations are often public enterprises such as museums, art galleries, theatre centres, and as such are open to public scrutiny, debate, and questioning. No more articulate and persistent critics exist than academics, artists, musicians, and other such professionals. It says much for our society that highly responsible people are willing to serve on these boards and, in many cases, work very diligently for their organization without compensation and often in the face of considerable criticism.

III

Since all corporations must have a board of directors, one is led to ponder why this is so. Could those who conceived or revised the law possibly have foreseen the incredible variety and multiplication of corporations that would evolve? Could any one set of principles possibly apply to this vast number of corporations, each of which is different in some respect to the others? Should directors have the same role and responsibility in each?

Is it possible to find within the law some general principles that explain the rationale for corporate structures requiring boards of directors which have certain responsibilities in common, regardless of other differences? It is to postulate, of course, but is it not reasonable to expect that those who created, wrote, and legislated corporate law in the western world would be influenced by the emerging philosophy and practices of their day? Specifically, they would be affected by new interpretations of democratic philosophy and the pragmatism that grew in western society from the days of the Industrial Revolution.

If one accepts this thesis, one can readily identify three principles that provided the guidelines for establishing corporate structure:

1) *Power must be decentralized:* There has always been the fear in democratic societies that too much power might be centralized in one person and/or one organization. Our government institutions reflect this as do our anti-monopoly and a variety of other laws. The ideal (if not the practice) was that power in the profit (and frequently in the non-profit) corporation should be distributed between shareholders (in non-profit corporations, members), a board of directors, and management. Again ideally, no one person could by him/herself control the destinies of a corporation, great or small. Any exercise of power required the approval, consent, and agreement of others. Thus was built into law the concept of the corporation as a limited democracy with a variety of voices having a say in how the corporation should operate.

2) *There should be a system of checks and balances:* Not only must power be dispersed, but also there must be built into the system a method by which conduct and activity could be monitored and judged by other than those directly involved. This is also an essential part of government structure in the western world and this idea or philosophy was undoubtedly influential in establishing corporate law. Thus, shareholders must approve board decisions as boards must approve certain management decisions. Management operates but the board and its committees carefully review these operations and report to the annual meeting of shareholders or members. The structure of a corporation provides for a system of checks and balances.

3) *There must be both rigidity and flexibility in the corporate structure:* Some balance between rigidity (some practices are unethical, immoral, or illegal and cannot be tolerated) and flexibility (in which creativity, experimentation, and new ideas are encouraged) is important in all societies and in all institutions. This also is a fundamental precept in western social philosophy as "human beings have a need

for structure and leadership as well as for freedom and self-determination."[6] Thus the law provides for a relatively rigid structure and minimum standards of conduct but it leaves the corporation relatively free to operate within these parameters. The corporation must have a board but, except for certain decisions only the board can make, the relationship of the board to management and the powers to delegate are left largely in the corporation's own hands. The by-laws of corporations reflect only part of the great variety of practices found within these organizations.

It may be pressing a case too far to suggest that these concepts provide a philosophy which should guide boards of directors in their work. Certainly such ideas are not often articulated and seem seldom to regulate corporate activity. Yet, if boards are to meet the criticisms hurled at them in present-day society, some consideration of basic principles might not be amiss. Is it too much to suggest that a reform should begin by reflecting on those ideas and values which are fundamental in our society?

---

[6]Neil H. Jacoby, *Corporate Power and Social Responsibility* (New York: Macmillan, 1973), p. 171.

The Layman and The Law
(PART ONE)

I

The law and its interpretation is for lawyers and the courts—not for laymen!

There is some justification for such an admonition because the law is not only complex, but is written in legal jargon difficult for the layman to understand, and with innumerable cross-references which defy all but the most patient. Then, too, the statutes and regulations are subject to change either by government action, or by decisions of the court which may interpret the law in a manner unanticipated by those who drafted the regulations. Very few laymen can expect to keep in touch with all developments in this highly specialized field.

Further, in Canada there are not only federal laws but provincial laws as well. Some corporations are incorporated in one of the provinces and must be aware of the particular laws of that province, while others are incorporated federally and must follow federal requirements. The Canada Business Corporations Act passed in 1975 to replace gradually the Canada Corporations Act, and to be the sole federal corporation act by December 1980, was the result of much deliberation and discussion at both the federal and provincial levels, with the hope of gradually bringing uniformity throughout the country to the laws governing corporations. But change is slow and there are still many significant differences between provinces which directors need to be aware of.[1] In such a simple matter as the tenure of directors, for example, "the federal Business Corporations Act provides that, if a director's term of office is not expressly stated it will terminate at the next annual meeting. The Ontario Act specifies that, if a company so provides in its articles, it can elect directors for a term of up to five years, while the Federal Act provides that a director can be elected for a term of three years. The British Columbia Act places no limitation on the terms of office of directors but Article 11.1 provides that the directors retire at each annual meeting."[2]

As already mentioned, there are special Acts in respect of banks, insurance companies, foundations, crown corporations, and many

[1]See Iacobucci, Pilkington, and Prichard, "Canadian Business Corporations," *Canada Law Book* (1977), pp. 226-340.

[2]Ibid, pp. 262-263.

non-profit corporations such as universities and hospitals. At least a careful reading of the Act under which an organization operates should be a minimum requirement for directors. Copies of these Acts are now readily available and, in many cases, summaries prepared by professional associations and accounting and legal firms. These summaries are generally reliable and readable and should not unduly challenge the intelligence of the non-legal director.[3]

One friend, recently appointed to the board of a bank, read the Bank Act before his first meeting. He came across a clause which indicated that not more than 20% of the directors of any company could sit on the same bank board. He was a member of another board which would have more than 20% of its directors on the board of the bank if he were to join. He was required by law to resign one of these two directorships—which he did. How many directors are this conscientious? One would guess not many! However, it illustrates that even a layman can understand law sufficiently to recognize danger signals which, in turn, can help him be a more useful director.

Nonetheless, each corporation should have a solicitor to advise and counsel on many issues which appear on the board agenda. No layman can hope to be aware of all the complexities of the law. Directors should have the right to seek the advice of the corporation's solicitor both within a meeting and outside. They should also have the right to ask for a second opinion if the issue being considered is extremely sensitive or important. Not all solicitors agree; they do not all interpret the law in the same way. Just as one may wish a second medical opinion before undergoing a serious operation, so boards should be free, without implying criticism of the corporation's solicitor, to seek further advice in matters of utmost importance.

II

However, in a fundamental sense, it is the responsibility of a director to be aware of the Act under which his board operates. The manager of a fighter usually refers to "we": "We were hurt in the seventh," "we was robbed," etc.—but it is the fighter alone who takes the punishment. Similarly lawyers identify with their clients: "We had a difficult day in court"—but it is the client alone who is on trial and who may bear the penalty. An intelligent responsible director should have some grasp of the law which governs his conduct and obligations as a director.

To illustrate, we will discuss a few sections of the new Canada

---

[3]See for example *Canada Business Corporations Act Summary of Highlights* (Toronto: Price Waterhouse & Co., 1977).

Business Corporations Act.[4] Anyone who has read the complete Act will know that there are some 266 sections in the Act, 23 sections dealing with Directors and Officers, 5 with Insider Trading, 14 with Shareholders, 8 with Proxies, 17 with Financial Disclosure, 18 with Fundamental Changes, 12 with Take-Over Bids, and many other sections which deal directly or indirectly with directors' duties. A careful reading of the whole Act is a formidable task and yet it is not without interest, for many sections of the Act are sufficiently ambiguous or challenging to stimulate speculation and discussion, not to mention sensitivity about one's responsibilities.

Perhaps the most important and controversial clause in the "Directors and Officers" is Section 97 which states: "Subject to any unanimous shareholder agreement the directors shall manage the business and affairs of the corporation." Now, the dictionary definition of "manage" is "to control and direct as a person or enterprise; to conduct, carry on, administer; to direct or conduct affairs, to carry on a concern or business." Very few directors of a large business or hospital or university would accept the idea that they could "manage" in this sense. The concept of management of any large enterprise by part-time directors is anathema to most.

Some lawyers and many directors choose to interpret "manage" as "monitor" (to maintain discipline and enforce rules of conduct) and this is, in fact, the maximum effort of most boards. Management—the actual operation of the enterprise—is left to appointed officers of the company.

The Canada Business Corporations Act provides for such delegation of authority (Section 110) by stating: "Directors of a corporation may appoint from among their number a managing director who is a resident Canadian or a committee of directors and delegate to such managing director or committee any of the powers of the directors." Notwithstanding this provision, there are many functions that cannot be so delegated: e.g., filling a vacancy among the directors, submitting to shareholders any question requiring the approval of shareholders, issuing securities except as authorized by the directors, declaring dividends, paying a commission to any person in consideration of the purchase of the company's shares, approving a take-over bid, approving a management proxy circular, approving a financial statement, adopting, amending, or repealing by-laws, etc. These and other similar actions are the responsibility of the board and cannot be subverted. Similarly, committees of the board (financial,

---

[4]All references to corporate law hereafter will refer to this Act unless otherwise specified.

audit, compensation, etc.) cannot act unilaterally without board approval unless such actions are provided for in the by-laws and approved by shareholders.

This, of course, raises the question of the degree to which directors can delegate responsibility and accountability. The board is elected "to manage," but as it cannot do this in any realistic manner, it is therefore permitted to delegate. The bothersome problem is the degree of responsibility it must accept not only for those duties specifically assigned to it but for the actions of those to whom it delegates. Part-time and volunteer directors can hardly be expected to have the time and the knowledge to make judgments about all aspects of a large complex organization. But one group of legal scholars say quite emphatically ". . . [directors] cannot delegate their decision-making powers over the most significant aspects of corporate management on which shareholders are entitled to expect the considered attention of all directors."[5] In the United States particularly, the courts seem to be holding the board responsible for actions clearly taken by management, but which may not have come to the board's attention.

The federal Act (Section 117) itself defines the responsibilities in very broad terms by stating that a director, in discharging his duties, shall (a) "act honestly and in good faith with a view to the best interests of the corporation" and (b) "exercise the care, diligence, and skill that a reasonably prudent person would exercise in comparable circumstances."

The conventional legal wisdom is that these provisions provide realistically for directors' liability. They cannot be expected to know everything that goes on in the large organization but if they are honest and exercise care, diligence, and skill, they have performed responsibly. Mr. Justice Romer (in the case of *City Equitable Fire Insurance Company*) said: "It is indeed impossible to describe the duty of directors in general terms, whether by way of analogy or otherwise. The position of a director of a company carrying on a small retail business is very different from that of a director of a railway company. . . . The larger the business carried on by the company the more numerous, and the more important, the matters that must be left to the managers, the accountants, and the rest of the staff."[6] He went on to say that where duties have been properly left to an official of the company, a director is, in the absence of grounds for suspicion, justified in trusting that official to perform the duties honestly. Directors, ac-

[5]Iacobucci *et al., op cit*, p. 280

[6]Quoted in *Ontario Corporation Law Guide Reports*, 31 August 1973, p. 5101.

cording to this widely quoted judgment, will thus be held liable for the misdeeds of officers and agents of the company only if they have been personally negligent or have acted unreasonably in relying on an official whose honesty or competence they have reasons to suspect.[7]

There are many corporate lawyers and directors who accept this interpretation of directors' responsibilities "to manage the business and affairs of the company." Certainly, it is a comforting one which relieves directors of legal liability if they exercise a minimum of prudence and skill. They are further protected, as Lewtas said, "by elaborate exculpatory provisions in articles and by-laws, which are probably effective except to the extent that they purport to condone fraud or come into conflict with specific statutory provisions."[8]

But it would be a mistake to consider the Romer judgment made in 1925 in Britain and ones similar to it made since then as likely to be acceptable and valid in the courts today or in the future. Our courts may have been slow to change but new ideas and attitudes are appearing. Legal scholars in our universities are now moving far beyond merely interpreting the law to examining the validity and relevance of the law in light of changing social attitudes and conditions. As Professor Stanley Beck, a well known authority on corporate law, has said: "Canada's highest courts and its most important Corporation Act have both fallen short of giving the leadership that is required to make the practice in the boardroom conform to the law in books"[9] and "the low standards of the common law—often accounts for directors' disappointing performance in practice."[10]

Fresh legal attitudes are now beginning to appear and new, higher standards for board behaviour are becoming evident, as will be seen in the court decisions discussed in the following chapter. Inevitably the law seems to follow public opinion. The latter is undoubtedly pressing for greater responsibility (and liability) for directors. This is reflected in a statement of Chief Justice Bora Laskin of the Supreme Court of Canada in which he said: "Strict application—against directors and senior management officials is simply recognition of the degree of control which their positions give them in corporate operations, *a control which rises above day-to-day accountability—an acknowledgement of the importance of the corporation in the life of the com-*

---

[7] Iacobucci *et al., op cit,* p. 288.

[8] Quoted in Jacobucci *et al,* p. 289.

[9] Ibid, p. 317.

[10] Ibid, p. 292.

munity and of the need to compel obedience by it and by its promo-
tors, directors, and managers to norms of exemplary behaviour"[11]
(italics mine).

Therefore, while up until the very recent past the law seemed to
allow directors a good deal of latitude and did not judge them too
harshly for daily management activities of the corporation, there is a
growing sentiment that the law has dealt far too casually with directors' responsibilities and that they must now be held to a much
stricter and more severe interpretation of their duties. A director
would be incautious to assume that the lenient attitude of the courts
in the past will prevail in the future.

Thus a simple phrase in the Act, "the directors shall manage the
business and affairs of the corporation," has caused difficulties in its
interpretation. Since the precise meaning of this phrase called for
what many considered an impossible obligation, lawyers and directors have diluted this directive to mean almost anything they
choose—the Romer decision providing an easy escape from onerous
and time-consuming duties. There are now new interpretations of the
term "to manage." It may not mean to operate in detail, but in the
view of one expert in this field it means: "The director must undertake the investigation, review, analysis, and examination necessary to
permit him to have adequate knowledge of the business and operations of the company, to provide appropriate supervision, guidance
and policy development—it is his responsibility to oversee the conduct of management, and the eye conducting such an examination
must be critical, but fair. . . ."[12] In the future the courts may be less
lenient in defining directors' duties.

III

If there is any question about the responsibilities or the duties of
directors "to manage," there should be none in respect of their fiduciary duties, i.e., their duties as trustees of the financial resources of
the corporation. Directors are responsible for managing the property
and the funds of the corporation, are comparable to trustees in terms
of the latter's duty to care for a trust fund, and are subject to the fiduciary requirement to act honestly, in good faith, with a view to the
best interests of the corporation.

One may well question whether certain directors' decisions have
been in the best interests of the corporation. The courts seem to have

---

[11] Ibid, p. 314.

[12] R. C. Brown, "The Legal Responsibilities of a Director" (Paper given at *Financial Post* Conference, Fall 1978).

been particularly lenient with directors of non-profit corporations, perhaps because these are volunteers who give their time to provide a particular service to the community. But it is not difficult to think of examples in which the boards of non-profit corporations have made decisions which an objective observer would call questionable in terms of the best interests of the corporation. In respect of profit corporations also, the courts have not been inclined to second-guess the wisdom of directors' judgments in business affairs.[13]

The traditional and established case law has tended to focus on "profit maximization" as the major, if not the sole, determining criterion in interpreting what constitutes "the best interests" of the profit corporation: on such a basis one could argue that directors should concentrate on profit above all else—including the interests of employees, creditors, customers, or society at large.[14] This is obviously a narrow, not to say out-dated, concept of what a director should do in a corporation that seeks to be "a good citizen." It should be said, however, that one legal authority advises: "Though some courts have demonstrated a willingness to broaden the profit maximization objective, the classical approach remains firmly established. In this state of the law, directors who depart from single-minded profit seeking are at considerable risk."[15]

This may be the judgment of one scholar—and it may even be the safest ground for the nervous director—but it flies in the face of modern developments. Where this to be an inflexible court opinion, directors of profit corporations might hesitate to make charitable donations or to take measures not required by law to improve the working and safety conditions of employees or to consider the implications of their decisions on the well-being of society. To suggest such considerations are of secondary or tertiary importance is to apply antiquated law which should be made obsolete. I very much doubt if the courts today, not to mention the near future, will be bound by such a limited and single-minded criterion of the best interests of the profit corporation.

There is, as is well known, a special obligation on directors to avoid conflict of interest situations. "As fiduciaries directors and officers are under a strict duty to avoid any conflict between self-interest and the interest of the corporation. Such conflicts may arise in several ways: an unscrupulous director or officer may use his position to gain ad-

---

[13]Iacobucci *et al, op cit.,* p. 295

[14]Ibid.

[15]Ibid, p. 296.

vantageous contracts or transactions with the corporation; he may divert to his own use opportunities of which he has become aware in his fiduciary capacity; he may use for his own purposes information entrusted to him as a fiduciary; he may compete with the corporation; or he may obtain a personal benefit in return for his co-operation in a take-over situation. These breaches of the fiduciary principle of loyalty are dealt with by the law in different ways: detailed statutory rules have been developed to regulate a director or officer's duty to disclose his interest in a corporate transaction and to regulate his use of confidential information in insider trading, but the other breaches are generally left to be governed by common law."[16]

Of major importance in this respect is that of disclosure in the light of possible conflict of interest. The law (Section 115) states: "A director or officer of a corporation who:

(a) is party to a material contract or proposal material contract with the corporation, or

(b) is a director or an officer of or has a material interest in any person who is party to a material contract or proposal material contract with the corporation, shall disclose in writing to the corporation or request to have entered in the minutes of meeting of directors the nature and extent of his interests."

This provision in itself does not prevent a conflict of interest; it merely requires that the conflict be noted and recorded and the director involved not participate in any resolution in respect of the conflict or possible conflict. Nonetheless Section 115 and subsequent paragraphs in the law clearly indicate that the person making such a declaration is marked as one who must be scrupulously honest and careful of his actions in respect of several corporations with which he or she may be associated.

There are some who feel that the fiduciary duties of directors have not been sufficiently detailed in statute and that the many possible dangers and penalties should be spelled out more clearly in the law. Thus Beck comments that "the impulse to enrichment through breach of fiduciary duty is strong," while at the same time there are "a number of factors that minimize the risk of detection and punishment for fiduciary wrong-doing." Directors are thus in "a tempting and difficult position and if a statutory statement of their duty has the salutary effect of making them more fully cognizant of and willing to comply with its requirements, then the statement is worth formulating."[17]

---

[16]Iacobucci *et al*, *op. cit.*, p. 300-301.

[17]Ibid, p. 314.

It is possible that in the near future the courts will examine much more closely and less leniently any breach or possible breach of fiduciary duties; that the courts will take a broader view of what constitutes "the best interests" of the corporation; and that in the long term the law may be altered to reflect these realities.

IV

There are other legal provisions about which many directors (exempting the corporation lawyers who sit on these boards) do not seem to be aware. For example, a director who resigns or is to be removed or replaced "is entitled to submit to the corporation a written statement giving the reasons why he opposes any proposed action or resolution" (Section 105) and "the corporation is required to send a copy of this statement to every shareholder entitled to receive notice of a shareholders meeting" (105-3). This is a most important entitlement, seldom used in Canada, which provides a dissenting director an opportunity to state his case and put it before the internal court of final decision, namely the shareholders. The authors of the Act see this as a provision that is in the interest not only of the director (who can state his case), but "also of the shareholders generally, since the removal power can obviously be used for both legitimate and illegitimate purposes."[18] Few corporations would wish such a confrontation; but in light of current values, conflicts, if they exist, should be open and not hidden under the boardroom table.

Some directors who miss one or more meetings operate under the illusion that they are not responsible for actions taken during their absence, but "A director who was not present at a meeting at which a resolution was passed or action taken is deemed to have consented thereto unless within seven days after he becomes aware of the resolution he (a) causes his dissent to be placed with the minutes of the meeting or (b) sends his dissent by registered mail or delivers it to the registered office of the corporation" (118-3).

This places an added burden not only on the absent director but also on the secretary of the corporation who is required by the implication of the previously mentioned Section to prepare detailed minutes that accurately reflect the actions of the board and to have these circulated promptly to board members. Minutes of board meetings tend not to be taken seriously; they will become much more important after the first court case in which a director seeks to prove he acted with prudence, care, and diligence but can find no support for such intent in any record of board meetings.

---

[18] Ibid, p. 267.

Another interesting Section, seemingly designed to confuse the average citizen, is one which disqualifies certain persons from being a director. The Act disqualifies "a person who is not an individual" (Section 100). This is, in fact, an important clause because in law a corporation is treated as a person and therefore a corporation could, if it were not for the condition stated above, act as a director—although it is clear that the corporation would have to be represented by an individual. This, of course, has wide ramifications in a country like Canada where there are many subsidiary corporations.

In the United States numerous companies allow cumulative voting in electing directors of the corporation. This is also permitted in Canada and under the new Act (Section 102) "each shareholder . . . has a right to cast a number of votes attached to the shares held by him multiplied by the number of directors to be elected, and he may cast all such votes in favor of one candidate. . . ." Cumulative voting is permitted if the articles and by-laws of the corporation call for such practice; *but cumulative voting is not required* and as yet is not a common practice here. But since the purpose of such voting is to provide minority shareholders an opportunity to obtain representation on the board by concentrating their votes, one may well see this method of voting gradually increase in both profit and non-profit corporations. The request by Brascan (a minority shareholder) to have Noranda introduce cumulative voting in 1980 may be an example of things to come. Still, it must be recognized that in closely held profit corporations the small shareholder has little chance of success.

Nonetheless shareholders are permitted to place their nominations before all the shareholders and this in itself could counter the power of management to control the proxy apparatus.[19] This right of nomination is enhanced for shareholders "holding not less than five per cent of the voting shares" by allowing them to submit nominations for the election of directors. If this is done 90 days before the anniversary date of the last annual meeting, the corporation that submits proxies "must include the nomination in or attach it to, the management proxy circular, together with any supporting statement of not more than two hundred words."[20] Thus the law seems to be moving toward, if not directly encouraging, greater opportunity for shareholders to participate in the affairs of the corporation.

There appears to be an attempt to "Canadianize" boards as is evident in several clauses of which the following is typical: "Directors—

---

[19]Ibid, p. 254.

[20]Ibid, p. 255.

shall not transact business at a meeting of directors unless a majority of directors present are resident Canadians" (Section 109-3). There are a number of clauses which condition this requirement: e.g., a Canadian director who is unable to attend a meeting but approves in writing or otherwise the business transacted at the meeting may be counted as being present; a corporation which earns in Canada less than five per cent of the gross revenues of the holding corporation and its subsidiaries is not required to have a majority of Canadian directors. There is a good deal of debate about the usefulness of these provisions in the Act—the nationalists say it does not go far enough since a multinational company can fill its Canadian board with Canadian employees, while others think this requirement an unnecessary nuisance in a business that is world-wide in scope. If the provisions in the Act are meant to assure a Canadian perspective in the boardroom, that which appears in the Act hardly guarantees such. More useful would be a requirement that a fixed percentage of board members be outsiders who are also Canadians.

Few directors seem aware that they have a liability to employees "for all debts not exceeding six months wages payable to each such employee for services performed for the corporation while they are such directors respectively" (Section 114). Of course there are exemptions. A director is not liable unless (1) the corporation has been sued for such debt within six months after it has become due and execution has been returned unsatisfied in whole or in part, or (2) the corporation has gone into liquidation, been dissolved, or has assigned or petitioned into bankruptcy and the claim for the debt has been proven. In addition, the director is liable only if he is sued while he is a director or within two years after he has ceased to be a director. The chances of such liability in most corporations, therefore, seems remote, yet the consequences of this minor passage are immense and cannot be ignored.

V

Perhaps one more illustration of the new legal requirements placed upon directors may not be amiss. A corporation planning to issue shares or debentures to the public must prepare a prospectus, the board being responsible for the contents. I am a director of such a corporation, and I received, as did all the directors, a letter from the corporation solicitor which warned: "The securities legislation of several of the provinces in which the prospectus is to be filed contain provisions to the effect that *if a material false statement is contained in a company's prospectus, each director of the company in office at the time of such filing is personally liable to compensate all purchasers of the securities offered thereunder for any loss or damage sustained by them as a result of their purchase.* A director will, however, not be liable under those provisions if he had reasonable grounds to believe and did believe the statement in question to be true or, in the case of an auditor's report or other statement of an expert contained or summarized in the prospectus, if he had no reasonable grounds to believe that the auditor or other expert was not competent to make the report or statement" (italics mine). There are "escape clauses" consistent with the Canada Business Corporations Act which allow a director exemption if he relies in good faith on (a) a financial statement represented to him by an officer or a written report of the auditor of the corporation or (b) a report by a lawyer, accountant, engineer, appraisee, or other person whose profession lends credibility to a statement made by him. But boards, including the one to which the above letter was sent, must ask detailed and searching questions of all these professionals and have these questions and the replies detailed in the minutes of the meeting if they are to fulfill their responsibilities and avoid liability.

Companies which go to the public for capital must be cognizant of the regulations of the various provincial security commissions. Perhaps the most important of these is the Ontario Securities Commission which has made an impressive review and study of security legislation and introduced a new Securities Act (September 15, 1979). The OSC report is an engrossing document with 118 pages of legislation and 1,816 pages of regulations. (Hardly a layman's idea of a pleasant evening's reading!)

But the Act is important for directors since it makes specific a framework of registering issuers, requires continuous disclosure, makes tougher civil liability provisions to all shareholders for better access to the courts, covers insider trading not only in the traditional sense but also for "tippees," i.e., people who have indirect contact with information and use it to advantage.

What is perhaps of most direct concern to directors is the requirement that companies which fall within the broad definition of a reporting issuer are required to keep OSC fully informed of their affairs, providing the Commission with regular reports including audited statements, quarterly reports to Ontario shareholders, notices of meetings with an information circular, and a timely press release whenever there is a material change in the affairs of the company.[21]

---

[21]"OSC in for busy time as new security rules go into effect," *The Globe and Mail*, 8 September 1979, p. B1.

Directors have in the past, as indicated above, tended to rely on reports by officers, lawyers, accountants, etc., to prepare such reports, and at first glance the requirement for a continuous flow of such information does not seem to be a burden. But under the new Act these experts or advisers (lawyers, accountants, officers) can be brought into court if, in a prospectus, take-over circular, or directors' circular, there has been a misrepresentation, untrue statement, or omission that would have a significant effect on share price. The implication of this is stated bluntly by James Baillie, the OSC Chairman:

"Some companies may well be surprised by the attitude of their advisers when they next enter the capital markets. They may find that their internal affairs are scrutinized with even greater care than has been the pattern in the past.

"Careful advisers . . . will wish to know *the procedures* in effect for corporate governance of the issuer. They will hope to be satisfied that those procedures are designed to provide adequate checks and balances and to avoid complete concentration of decision-making in the hands of a dominant chief executive officer."[22]

This is to say that corporate governance requires boards of directors who are elected to participate in and make decisions about the affairs of the corporation. "Dummy boards" or boards of "patsies" or "yes men" appear not to be acceptable. Proper corporate governance calls for an elected board of directors who have knowledge of the company and make decisions about its affairs as honest and prudent persons.

There have been few more heartening statements about the role of directors than that by Mr. Baillie. Implicit in it is the suggestion that boards of directors may have been somewhat less than alert, active, and responsible when major company decisions were being made in the past. While there is not in the Ontario Securities Act a legal requirement for a particular level of skill on the part of boards, still there is an underlying appeal to both advisers and directors to rise to high standards of participation.

VI

The previous examples illustrate some of the legal requirements of boards. They can in no way be considered comprehensive, complete, or technically valid. They are presented as a few of the conditions that interest one particular layman with the hope that directors will be stimulated to discuss the Acts and regulations which govern their boards and to ask many more specific questions of their corporate solicitor.

---

[22]James C. Baillie, "Steps to be taken by reporting issuers to comply with the Securities Act 1978" (Paper given at Insight Conference, September 24, 1979).

The Layman and The Law
(PART TWO)

I

The law is not an easy doctrine for the layman. It seems at times to be inconsistent or ambiguous, at other times unduly lenient, and at still other times extremely severe. Perhaps the most effective way to understand what is meant by the statements reviewed in Part One is to examine some recent court actions and decisions which illustrate how the courts interpret that which may seem confusing to the layman.

We can be almost certain of two things. First, there will be far more legal actions taken against boards of directors. The number of such actions in the United States has multiplied rapidly in recent years and, if Canada follows the United States, as it seems often to do in such matters, we can expect many more court cases here. There are already indications of this: the actions by two shareholders against Brascan[1] and by a shareholder against Maple Leaf Mills,[2] the $525-million-suit by two stockholders against Canadian Pacific,[3] the publicity given to the resignation of George E. Creber as President of Consumers' Gas and the questions raised about his board's responsibility in respect of his actions as "management."[4] The prominence given by the media to minority shareholders' questions and attacks aimed at Pop Shoppes,[5] Talcorp,[6] Falconbridge,[7] and the proposed merger of Metropolitan Trust and Victoria and Grey Trust[8] also attest to a trend to hold directors accountable. All of these, as well as other suits and potential actions, must be a warning to Canadian directors to be scrupulous in meeting their obligations as members of boards.

---

[1] *The Globe and Mail,* 8 May 1979, p. 38.

[2] (1979), 22 *Ontario Reports* (2d).

[3] *The Financial Post,* 24 September 1979, p. 3.

[4] *The Financial Post,* 7 April 1979, pp. 1, 10.

[5] "Minority Shareholders Attack Pop Shoppe's Practices," *The Globe and Mail,* 29 June 1979, p. B6.

[6] "Shareholder Assails Talcorp Plant . . .," *The Globe and Mail,* 30 March 1979, p. B8.

[7] "Falconbridge Chief Dodges T.V. Cameras . . .," *Toronto Star,* 12 April 1979, p. E12.

[8] "Shareholders Fight Merger . . .," *The Financial Post,* 21 July 1979, p. 24.

The other apparent trend is that the law is likely to be more strictly interpreted and that directors will be judged by standards far higher than those expected of the ordinary citizen. Mr. Justice Cardozo expressed this clearly in dealing with an important case in the United States. "Many forms of conduct permissible in a workaday world for those acting at arm's length, are forbidden to those bound by fiduciary ties. A trustee is held to something stricter than the morals of the market place. *Not honesty alone but a punctillio of an honour the most sensitive, is then the standard of behaviour.* As to this there has developed a tradition that is unbending and inveterate. Uncompromising rigidity has been the attitude of courts of equity when petitioned to undermine the rule of undivided loyalty . . . only thus has the level of conduct for fiduciaries been kept at a level higher than that trodden by the crowd"[9] (italics mine). As we will see, this view of directors' duty is being accepted in Canadian courts.

II

A very enlightening judgment was given by Chief Justice Bora Laskin in what we shall call here the *Canadian Aero Service Ltd.* (hereafter *Canaero*) case.[10] It is an action that is interesting in itself but its importance is not simply the problem of directors' conduct, nor the differences in the decision of the lower and higher courts, but Chief Justice Laskin's exploration and clear exposition of the duties of directors in the Canadian context.

Very briefly, Canaero sued two of its senior officers (the President and Executive Vice-President), who were inside directors, and one outside director (who had resigned a year before the action) for improperly taking "the fruits of a corporate opportunity in which Canaero had a prior and continuing interest." Canaero (a U.S.-owned firm) had been seeking a government contract to do topographical mapping and aerial photography of parts of Guyana. This was to be financed by an External Aid grant or loan from the government of Canada. While this contract was being pursued by Canaero through the two officers mentioned above, the Executive Vice-President resigned on August 19, 1966, and, on the advice of the former outside director, incorporated a new company (Terra Surveys Limited) on August 16, 1966. This company sought, and in November 1966 se-

---

[9]Quoted in Vincent Powell-Smith, *The Law and Practice Relating to Company Directors* (London: Butterworths, 1969), pp. 126-127.

[10]Canaero v. O'Malley, *Supreme Court Reports*, 1974, p. 592.

cured, the contract for the survey mentioned above, for the sum of $2,300,000.

To most businessmen, the action of these two officers was unfair, perhaps even dishonourable. The fact that they resigned, formed a company, and took over part of the business of their former company, appears to be, on the surface at least, an unethical action. But the relevant question is whether such action was illegal? What is perhaps surprising is the difference of opinion in the various courts in which the case was tried.

In the first instance, in the lower court, Canaero failed to win its case and this judgment was upheld by the Court of Appeal. In other words, the courts held that these officers and directors did not act illegally. However, this judgment was reversed before the Supreme Court, the defendant inside directors were found guilty, but the action against the outside director, who had resigned a year before, was dismissed.

The differences in the judgments of the two courts is revealing for it suggests some lack of clarity in the law about the responsibility of officers and directors of corporations. What is most important to remember, however, is that the final decision to find for Canaero was made by the Supreme Court and that this judgment and the reasoning leading to it have been and will continue to be widely quoted and used as a basis for other actions against directors.

The defence argued that the proposal of the new company varied from that of Canaero, that the principals had acted with honesty of purpose, that Canaero would not in any case have received the contract, etc. All these defences Chief Justice Laskin dismissed: "In my opinion, the fiduciary duty upon O'Malley and Zarzycki, if it survived their departure from Canaero, would be reduced to an absurdity if it could be evaded merely because the Guyana project had been varied in some details. . . ."[11] and "whether or not Terra was incorporated for the purpose of intercepting the contract for the Guyana project is not central to the issue of breach of fiduciary duty. Honesty of purpose is no more a defence in that respect than it would be in respect of personal interception of the contract by O'Malley and Zarzycki. This is fundamental in the enforcement of fiduciary duty where the fiduciaries are acting against the interests of their principal."[12] And "since Canaero had been invited to make a proposal on the Guyana project, there is no basis for contending that it could not,

---

[11] Ibid, p. 616.

[12] Ibid, p. 617.

in any event, have obtained the contract or that there was any un-willingness to deal with it."[13]

Judgment was therefore in favour of the plaintiff: "[Canaero] is en-titled to compel the faithless fiduciaries to answer for their default ac-cording to their gain. . . . The appeal is, accordingly, allowed against all defendants save Wells, and judgment should be entered against them for $125,000."[14]

There are many strong phrases in this judgment which the alert reader will note with care: certain arguments can be reduced "to an absurdity," "honesty of purpose is no defence," and "faithless fidu-ciaries," to mention but three. In cumulative form Mr. Justice Laskin served notice not only on the defendants in this case, but also on all officers and directors, of a higher and more demanding standard of duty than had previously been the case in Canada.

In speaking of the new ethic to be applied to directors he said: ". . . a strict ethic in this area of the law . . . disqualifies a director or senior officer from usurping for himself or diverting to another per-son or company with whom or with which he is associated a matur-ing business opportunity which his company is actively pursuing; he is also precluded from so acting even after his resignation where the resignation may fairly be said to have been prompted or influenced by a wish to acquire for himself the opportunity sought by the com-pany, or where it was his position with the company rather than a fresh initiative that led him to the opportunity which he later ac-quired."[15]

This is certainly a clear statement and a clear warning of the degree to which directors must exercise the greatest care to avoid any situa-tion in which they may, deliberately or not, attain a material advan-tage because of the position they hold as corporate directors.

Mr. Justice Laskin underlines this point by stating: "The reaping of a profit by a person at a company's expense while a director is, of course, an adequate ground upon which to hold the director account-able. Yet *there may be situations where a profit must be disgorged, although not gained at the expense of the company*, on the ground that a director must not be allowed to use his position as such to make a profit if it was not open to the company, as for example, by reason of legal dis-ability"[16] (italics mine).

I take this to mean that if the board of McGraw-Hill Ryerson de-

---

[13]Ibid, p. 619.
[14]Ibid, p. 622.
[15]Ibid, p. 607.
[16]Ibid, p. 609.

cides to purchase a periodical or TV station, but discovers it is forbidden by law to make such a purchase, I as a director am not allowed either by myself, or with others, to purchase what may seem to be an excellent business opportunity unless it is clear that McGraw-Hill Ryerson has formally announced it has terminated its interest in this project.[17] It is only when one faces such practical situations that one begins to be aware of the restrictions of law that may be placed upon directors.

What exactly this law means will become apparent as more detailed judgments are made in Canadian courts. We have tended to rely on former court decisions, particularly those in Britain (such as the 1925 Romer decision), but it is possible that our own courts will give fresh interpretations and new leadership to corporate law. In the judgment we are discussing, Chief Justice Laskin indicated that prior court decisions could not be considered as "the exclusive touchstones of liability. In this as in other branches of the law, new fact situations may require a reformulation of existing principle to maintain its vigour in a new setting."[18]

As suggested earlier, the *Canaero* case is less important for the specific problem with which it deals than for the courts' exploration of the obligations and duties of officers and directors. The language and its intent in this judgment seem to imply a very strict interpretation of the responsibility of persons holding these positions. It very clearly calls for a standard of conduct far above that of the ordinary citizen and "not honesty alone, but a punctillio of an honour the most sensitive, is the standard of behaviour."

III

It may be useful to consider the famous *BarChris* case, for while it occurred in the United States, legal opinion in Canada is sensitive to its application here. It is particularly important for "outside directors," who may feel somewhat less responsible for corporate activity than directors who are also officers of the corporation.

BarChris was a bowling alley construction company that sold convertible debentures to the public, later defaulted on the payment of interest, and filed for bankruptcy.[19] It was charged by holders of the

---

[17]Of three lawyers to whom I made this statement, one agreed and two dissented.

[18]Canaero v. O'Malley, *op cit.*, p. 609.

[19]Much of the material about this case comes from Jeremy Bacon and James K. Brown, *Corporate Directorship Practices: Role, Selection and Legal Status of the Board* (New York: The Conference Board, Inc., 1975), pp. 84-86.

debentures that the registration statement (comparable to a Canadian prospectus) contained false statements and omissions.

The court concluded that there were "various misstatements and omissions: overstatement of sales, gross profit, and backlog of customer orders; and failure to disclose the true facts regarding borrowing from officers; the anticipated use of the proceeds from debentures; customer deficiencies and BarChris potential liability with respect to them; and BarChris potential involvement in operation of bowling alleys, a function it would undertake only when a customer was in default."[20] Are there any other mistakes a board could possibly make? In any case the directors, who included five officers of the company and four outside directors (an attorney, a partner in an underwriting firm, a banker, a civil engineer), were tried on these charges.

Each director claimed that with respect to portions of the registered statement, he depended on the authority of an expert—an officer, an accountant, a lawyer; on the other parts of the statement he exercised "due diligence," since he had reasonable grounds to believe that the statement was true and no facts had been omitted.

The court rejected the defence of four of the five officer-directors because of their intimate knowledge of the company which should have provided them with ability to judge the accuracy of both the expertized and unexpertized parts of the statement.

What is of greater significance is that the court decided that while the outside directors and one officer-director should justifiably be able to rely on the financial data prepared by independent accountants ("expertized information"), these five directors had failed to exercise due diligence in respect of other parts of the statement and were therefore liable. This is placing far more responsibility on outside directors than they have been accustomed to bearing.

Very significant also is the judgment in respect of the two new directors (the banker and the civil engineer). Both had become directors *after* the first registration statement was filed. Both had investigated BarChris before accepting a position on the board and both had received favourable reports on the company. When they signed the form of the registration they relied, as did other outside directors, on management, accountants, and lawyers. Neither read the statement thoroughly nor made an independent investigation.

One might expect the court to be less severe on these new directors. But the court said to them: "Section 11 imposes liability in the first instance upon a director no matter how new he is. He is pre-

---

[20] Ibid.

sumed to know his responsibility when he becomes a director. He can escape liability only by using that reasonable care to investigate the facts which a prudent man would employ in the management of his own property. In my opinion, a prudent man would not act in an important matter without any knowledge of the relevant facts, in sole reliance upon representations of persons who are comparative strangers and upon general information which does not purport to cover the particular case. To say that such minimal conduct measures up to the statutory standard would, to all intents and purposes, absolve new directors from responsibility merely because they are new. This is not a sensible construction of Section 11 when one bears in mind its fundamental purpose of requiring full and truthful disclosure for the protection of investors. . . ."[21]

This case is of considerable interest to Canadians since our law allows directors to rely on "expert opinion" unless there are grounds to doubt the reliability of such opinion. Generally directors have been able to justify their actions on the basis of the advice and reports presented to them by company officers, accountants, lawyers, engineers, etc. But the *BarChris* judgment places much greater emphasis on the reasonable care that a prudent man would take in such an important matter. It suggests that a diligent person in dealing with a personal transaction, in which a large amount of money was involved, would not rely entirely on reports presented to him by corporate representatives, but would investigate these reports carefully, probably seeking "a second opinion" on some issues about which he had questions. If he would exercise such care in personal transactions, he should do so also in the affairs of a corporation of which he is a director.

The implication is that the obligation, honesty, care, diligence, prudence, etc., required of directors cannot always be by-passed by an "expert opinion." What is suggested is that when very far-reaching decisions are to be made, the director should not only review the whole situation with care but question closely those experts upon whose reports he must rely. If this view of the law is to prevail in Canada, directors will be required to seek much more information and to give much more time to board decisions than has been the case in the past.

IV

Another case, unprecedented in Canadian law, concerned Maple Leaf Mills. Until recently, minority shareholders who disagreed with

---

[21]Ibid, pp. 85-86.

the actions of the board or actions of the majority had few options except to protest and/or sell their shares. Under new legislation, where a shareholder disagrees with decisions about a transfer of shares or a merger with another company, he can force the corporation to buy back his shares at "fair value" by filing a notice of dissent before a shareholders' vote is taken.[22] A minority shareholder of Maple Leaf Mills recently took advantage of this provision in a manner which cost the company and its directors considerable embarrassment—not to mention financial considerations.

What was proposed was an amalgamation of Maple Leaf Mills with its parent company, Norin Canada Holdings Inc.—an Ontario company 100% owned by Norin Corporation, a U.S. public corporation.[23] Maple Leaf had only one class of shares, 94.5% of which were owned by Norin Canada. The purpose of the proposed change was to make Maple Leaf Mills a wholly owned subsidiary of Norin U.S. What the corporation proposed was that the minority shareholders be given a non-voting preference share on a one-to-one basis for each common share, the preference share to be redeemable at $18 per share or at some other redemption amount to be determined by arbitration. A meeting of shareholders was called to approve this proposal and a minority shareholder sued for an injunction to prevent such a meeting, under various heads, but specifically that the amalgamation was unlawful and contrary to the Ontario Business Corporations Act.

In commenting on the case Mr. Justice Steele said: ". . . the application before me would appear to be the first of its nature that has come before the Courts."[24] For this reason his judgment on this matter is of considerable import. One of the questions he raised was "whether or not the directors have breached a fiduciary responsibility to the applicants. I hasten to say that I certainly find no indication of fraud or any indication of malevolent interest on the part of the directors, and my comment with respect to the fiduciary relationship is strictly whether such exists in law or not."[25]

Indeed the hearing showed clearly that full disclosure had been made and the matter had been cleared with the Ontario Securities Commission, but it is of interest to note that the court concerned itself

---

[22]Peterson, *op. cit.*, p. 117.

[23]Carlton Realty Co. Ltd. et al. vs. Maple Leaf Mills Ltd. et al. (1979), 22 O.R. (2d) 198.

[24]Ibid, p. 199.

[25]Ibid, p. 205.

with directors' responsibilities and not simply the issue of corporate activity.

Mr. Justice Steele held for the plaintiff (the minority shareholder) and issued an injunction preventing the special meeting of shareholders. In his judgment the Justice stated that the proposed amalgamation would deprive the minority group of their common shares and replace them with preferred shares which could be redeemed at the will of the corporation. "There is no power for this Corporation to redeem its shares directly and *there is no provision in the Business Corporation Act (Ontario) that specifically provides for the squeezing out of minority shareholders*" (italics mine).

It was obviously a difficult decision to make and there are indications that Mr. Justice Steele struggled with issues that were new in Canadian courts. Referring to a judgment in a similar U.S. case, he suggested that "it was sufficient if the applicant satisfied the Court that his case was not a frivolous one and that there was a substantial issue to be tried;" stating his own view on this he said: "[T]here is a burden upon the applicant to show the Court that he has enough of a case—that when it comes to trial he will have a reasonable chance of success."[26] Thus the Judge implied that the Court would not entertain or tolerate frivolous or "nuisance" charges by minority shareholders and that the latter must have sufficient grounds to make a strong case when and if a trial were held. One would assume that in granting an injunction, he was convinced that in the case of Maple Leaf Mills, the minority shareholder had such a case.

Following the injunction Maple Leaf Mills and each of its directors were sued by Carlton—the minority shareholder. The case was settled out of court and while the amount of the settlement is not apparently in the public domain, private reports are that the total cost to the company was very considerable.

As already suggested this case is of importance both for minority shareholders and for directors. The former may take action in the courts on some matters heretofore considered not open to them, but it is clear that such actions can only be taken when their action can reasonably be expected to be supported by law. There must be sound grounds for appearing before the court. For all directors, who in this case seemed to act honestly and with prudence, there is cause to be increasingly vigilant about all board actions. The interests of minority shareholders, and not simply the interests of the controlling shareholder, must be considered and respected in major company moves.

---

[26] Ibid, p. 202.

In spite of the legal actions previously described, one cannot say the law in respect of directors is clear and unambiguous. In his judgment of this same case Mr. Justice Steele said: "I am of the opinion that a Judge must weigh the degree of harm against the difficulty of assessing such harm in coming to his conclusion. He should not be bound by any iron-clad rule set up by semantics of phrases. Again the balance of convenience must be weighed carefully as well as the desirability of maintaining the *status quo*—Justice is something that no two people including no two Judges will ever agree upon exactly. Unfortunately that is the very nature of the discretionary remedy."[27]

V

Many actions against corporations are settled out of court. Not only is a court action often time-consuming and expensive, but also the nature of the evidence, the court's decision, and the media's treatment of it are unpredictable.

An example of this is Imperial Oil's action against Nova Scotia Power and Light Company for not making payments for crude deliveries as Imperial interpreted their contract with Nova Scotia Power to require. The amount of money involved was approximately $100,000,000.[28]

In some respects the case was a simple one which required only that the court pass judgment on the meaning of "increase in tax," a phrase in the contract which Imperial claimed was an escalation clause that allowed them to pass on an increase in the price of Venezuelan oil to its customer, Nova Scotia Power. There was debate about the proper name of the Venezuelan increase—was it a price increase? a royalty? a tax? The court held that the tax referred to in the contract was meant, and was understood by Nova Scotia Power, to refer to a Canadian or provincial tax. The judge's decision, upheld by the Supreme Court of Nova Scotia and the Supreme Court of Canada, was: "The plaintiff [Imperial] will not be entitled to increase the agreed price to reflect changes in the amount of the Venezuelan Government take since they do not fall within the meaning of Clause 9 of the agreement."[29]

This statement over-simplifies the issue which was debated with zest and skill by lawyers on both sides. The point to be made here is

---

[27]Ibid, pp. 203-204.

[28]Imperial Oil Limited v. Nova Scotia Light and Power Company Limited, Supreme Court of Nova Scotia, Trial Division, 1971, S.C. No. 17812, p. 216.

[29]Ibid, p. 264.

that at first glance the issue seemed focused on a very specific issue and, indeed, the courts scrupulously avoided judgment on any other issue. But, inevitably, much information emerged about Imperial Oil that might give comfort to its competitors and/or its critics.

It was stated in the judgment, for example, that Imperial secured its Venezuelan oil through subsidiaries of its own or of Exxon (its parent company) and that there was price change as it passed from company to company. "The evidence indicates that the price of crude paid by Imperial to Albury was market price. Thus the price paid by Albury to Creole was 10¢ below market. This amount was never in fact passed on by Imperial to the respondent. Albury paid it back to Imperial by way of tax-free dividends. Mr. Pugsley argued that this was a device used for two reasons—(1) to escape income tax in Canada and (2) to escape income tax in Venezuela."[30]

There is little in the court's decision to suggest that these various companies and the degree of control of oil distribution by Exxon was anything but complicated. There was no pronouncement of illegal activity.

But for those who followed the court proceedings from the outside, there was a quite different reaction—a judgment that Exxon's and Imperial's activities, if not illegal, were at least questionable. *The New York Times* reviewed this case in detail and reported in bold print on its front page: "The litigation disclosed that Exxon occasionally backdates agreements in order to pass along more costs, disguised increases in company profit margins and knowingly gave out inaccurate information to customers, resulting in higher prices. All this was conceded in testimony by Exxon officials or substantiated by Exxon documents entered into evidence."[31] A few months after this report, questions about Imperial and Exxon were raised in the House of Commons in Ottawa. There may yet be more publicity about it.

The point to be emphasized here is that one cannot predict the course of events in court proceedings. What seemed here to be a relatively clear-cut action by Imperial, relating to a difference of opinion, led to media reports which can hardly be said to improve the public image of Exxon and Imperial.

The lesson is that corporations must at all times be prepared for full disclosure of all of their activities. Such disclosure may come directly or indirectly through court action. A board member cannot sit com-

---

[30] Imperial Oil Limited v. Nova Scotia Light and Power Company Limited, Supreme Court of Nova Scotia, Appeal Division, 1971, S.C., No. 17812, p. 23.

[31] "Exxon Records in Canadian Trial Point to Artificially High Oil Price," *The New York Times*, 30 September 1979, pp. 1, 46.

fortably in the belief that certain activities of the corporation are hidden or unlikely ever to be revealed. When it strikes, as it may at any time, the law will demand full disclosure.

VI

These briefly reviewed judgments may or may not represent the wave of the future. There are many who dismiss them as being unusual, unlikely to happen in well-managed corporations, and since most directors bring good judgment and honesty to the boardroom, they have little to fear. There may be some validity in these arguments. But they ignore three facts that emerge from our examination of the law.

1) *The law has changed:* The Canada Business Corporations Act, in spite of its ambiguities and its many clauses of exemptions, was clearly designed to enforce higher standards of conduct on corporations and their directors. This Act may have its weaknesses but it requires more responsibility of directors than the Act it replaced. Nonetheless there are those who think the new Act does not demand too much but that it demands too little! As such, the future is not for directors who dismiss as irrelevant the deepest probing of corporate activity; it is for directors who insist on complete information, disclosure, and discussion, and adequate time for decision making.

2) *The courts will be less lenient than in the past:* If the actions discussed are any indication, the courts are unlikely to overlook serious errors because those who made them were honest, sincere, only part-time directors, trusted the judgment of experts, etc. The court will more likely examine in detail not only the decisions and actions of directors, but will also concern itself with the process that led to these decisions and actions. Were they preceded by complete information, full disclosure, etc.? There may well be less opportunity to hide behind some of the many exemptions the law seems to provide.

3) *The media, minority shareholders, and pressure groups are more observant of board behaviour than in the past:* One only needs to note the number of shareholders and the number of union or staff protests publicized by the media, and the number of editorials relating to board activity, to recognize that in recent years the boardroom, if not open, is at least subject to scrutiny by many eyes. The issue is not whether all criticisms are justified; it is that board behaviour is monitored as never before. This being the case, directors must be certain they can justify their decisions.

Peterson's study of "50 prominent members of the business community"[32] in Canada suggests that some directors are living in the past, either ignoring or ignorant of the changing social situation, while others are alert, sophisticated, and moving to make changes consistent with new laws and new public expectations of board activity. The future would seem to belong to the latter. As one student of board activity has said: "The body of law is slowly forming itself to focus on the personal liability for directors when they do not carry out their duties."[33]

---

[32] Peterson, *op. cit.*

[33] Mueller, *op. cit.*, p. 4.

Beyond The Law— The Duties of Directors

I

The law provides the fundamental guide for a director. But he is left to ask how he should act as an honest and prudent person to deal with the many issues and problems with which a corporation is inevitably faced. Further he must recognize that he is elected as a director not merely to fulfill the legal obligations of the Board but also to make a contribution to the well-being of the corporation. He is not to be a neutral symbol, but a positive force in the life of the corporation. And, if he is at all sensitive, he will acknowledge that the current social climate requires him to consider the impact of corporate activity and board decisions on the larger community.

Thus, directors' duties are multiple and, at first glance, appear to be so broad and general in nature that they may seem to be little more than meaningless symbols. Fortunately there has developed in recent years, through discussion and conference, a fairly clear outline of the specific tasks a board should undertake if directors are to do all that is implied in the preceding paragraph.

These duties are, of course, stated in a variety of ways; so much so that one cannot say there is any one document which is held up as *the* guideline. Mueller,[1] for example, suggests directors should be prepared to score the corporation on criteria that include such factors as (1) financial position, such as return on stockholders equity, return on investment, return on sales; (2) the management of assets; (3) development of succession and good organization structure and practice; (4) creation of new products (or services); (5) organization climate; (6) corporate identity and image; (7) growth potential; (8) share of market; (9) willingness to have divestments as well as acquisitions; (10) research and development policy; (11) international position.

These and other such statements are valuable guidelines, yet they often lack the specificity that many directors seem to seek. I have, therefore, developed my own list of duties and attempt to clarify them by illustrating examples. The list has been reviewed by a

---

[1]Mueller, *op cit.*, p. 80.

number of directors, all of whom agree that if directors performed all the functions herein outlined, they would indeed be acting as the law and the public require.

Before I detail the criteria I have in mind for board activity, a special word should be said about non-profit corporations. Many of these operate under the Canada Business Corporations Act and others under special Acts that are equally demanding. As one student of corporate law says: "In many ways, non-profits are the most undaunted by present law, sometimes through the special immunities they enjoy, sometimes because of judicial sympathy, and sometimes because their management is further removed from profit constraints than the management of business corporations [although the differences are not nearly as striking as the terminological between 'for profit' and 'not for profit' would suggest]. For example, the financial management of nonprofits is notoriously bad; all the reasons for requiring say, independent audit committees on corporations listed on the stock exchanges would seem to apply all the more forcefully to some of our giant charities."[2] I have in mind both profit and non-profit corporations in the responsibilities listed below.

II

1) *Goal and Policy Determination:* The board is responsible for establishing both long-term and short-term goals for the corporation. This is not to say that management does not formulate these goals and objectives but, if this is the practice, automatic approval by the board should not be expected. The board has an obligation to explore, question, and change, if necessary, any such plans presented by the Chief Executive Office (CEO).

In the mid-1960s Imperial Oil "shifted its focus from oil exploration in the western provinces to three major projects: (1) large gas and oil fields in Canada's frontier lands and in the Arctic, (2) trying to develop crude-bearing heavy oil sands, and (3) drilling offshore along the nation's east coast. Imperial executives were particularly enamoured of the notion that vast resources lay in the High Arctic and Mackenzie Delta areas."[3] Such a major shift in objectives in any corporation is unquestionably of the greatest importance and should not be made without considerable research and discussion by management. Further, it should not take place without detailed consideration by the board, and only with board approval.

[2] Christopher D. Stone, "Controlling Corporate Misconduct," *The McKinsey Quarterly,* Winter 1978, p. 68.

[3] *Business Week,* 20 November 1978, pp. 125-126.

J. Herbert Smith, when Chairman of the DeHavilland Board of Directors, took the initiative in drafting a set of company objectives which was approved by officers and directors of the company. A close reading of these objectives makes clear their importance in providing essential guidelines for the corporation both in the long term and in the near future:

COMPANY OBJECTIVES

(1) *General*

–To develop a long term financially viable, distinctive, Canadian Aerospace Company that is competitive internationally in markets and with products carefully selected in relation to the innovative and economic utilization of Canadian skills and resources.

–To establish and maintain a position of pre-eminence in the selected products and markets so as to provide a base for a nationally integrated aerospace industry should that become a national policy.

–To restrict the product and service scope of the Company to the aerospace industry and to those areas where its aerospace technology provides a unique advantage.

(2) *Specific*

(1) Continue to develop and maintain the innovative design and manufacturing capability required to hold world leadership position in STOL aircraft for both civilian and military applications.

(2) Employ the skills utilized in attaining STOL leadership in seeking out and developing other profitable unique aerospace product lines in which comparable international recognition can be earned.

(3) Employ the same skills in seeking out and developing profitable aerospace and directly related sub-contracting work, or the manufacturing and marketing of aerospace and directly related component products.

(4) Continue to develop and maintain the required product planning expertise required to identify changing market needs and to translate these needs into product specifications utilizing in-place or available design and manufacturing capability in order to continue to successfully market the above product lines.

(5) Continue to develop and maintain the international marketing organization required to sell and service military and civilian users, worldwide.

(6) Base the long-term business strategy on earning a 20% return, before interest and corporate taxes, on the total funds employed.

A small hospital in the north established as its objective "(1) to build a 20 bed hospital for emergency, for obstetrical care, and for patients too ill to be cared for at home, and (2) to develop cooperative and coordinated arrangements with the P_____ General Hospital [a hospital in a nearby city] so that patients requiring major surgery, psychiatric, orthopedic or other specialized care can be sent by our physicians and nurses to the Hospital for immediate attention."[4] This too is board-established objective, in which doctors and nurses undoubtedly had input but which is clearly a decision of lay board of directors.

A report on Atomic Energy of Canada Ltd. suggests the difficulties a corporation may face if its goals are not clearly stated and understood: "More by accident than design, it changed from a research orientated corporation to a marketing or commercial organization" and moved into a highly competitive market to sell Candu reactors. "Lacking marketing expertise and adequate financial management AECL stumbled into problems that could have been avoided had anyone been monitoring the Crown corporation's dealing." The President of the Corporation hired a representative of AECL (at a fee later established at $20 million) and "three months after Mr. Gray [the President] had officially retained Mr. Eisenberg [the agent], the agent's name was first mentioned at a meeting of the AECL's Board of Directors".[5] Assuming this is an accurate report, it provides an example of very inadequate communication between management and the board of directors, of a management probably going beyond the limits of its authority, and of a board not sufficiently aware of its objectives or alert to its obligations. Here we must note that there appeared to be no clear goals or objectives established by which management should or could be guided and monitored by the board.

Most would agree that corporations should have long-term objec-

---

[4] Private memo in which anonimity was requested since the policy is now undergoing change.

[5] "A success story, but . . ." Geoffrey Stevens, *The Globe and Mail*, 4 February 1977, p. 6.

tives that are to be achieved over many years. In addition many corporations have five-year plans[6] and almost all have (or should have) one-year goals. In profit-making companies these include projections of sales, expenses, profit margins, acquisitions, restructuring of the organization, marketing strategy, etc., often broken down by divisions in the corporation so that standards of measurement are available for various parts of the company. Non-profit corporations may use different terms but each needs a budget plan that will set forth objectives for the year and the costs involved.

Such plans should be presented and discussed at board meetings. In this new era the board must insist that both long- and short-term objectives be openly and frankly studied. The board must then make a decision about them and, while it may delegate to staff the task of carrying out these plans, it has some responsibility to see they are implemented. Indeed, the plans established provide criteria for measuring management results.

The board also has responsibility for policy decisions. Some aspects of policy—the manner in which the corporation is to operate—are contained in the by-laws (this will be discussed later). There are two more kinds of policy decisions. One is a general policy statement outlining the board's position with respect to its purposes, intent, and practices. McGraw-Hill, Inc., has published for all its employees a "Code of Business Ethics" in which it describes the background and nature of the company, "what employees have a right to expect of McGraw-Hill," "what McGraw-Hill has a right to expect of us as employees," and "what the public has a right to expect of McGraw-Hill and its staff." The statement is, of necessity, in broad general terms, yet it is of great importance for all concerned that it contains, for example, sentences such as: "The privacy of your personnel and payroll records will be respected, and you have a right to examine these records yourself," and "An employee should never become involved in a situation with a supplier that could possibly be interpreted as improper. Certainly no payment or other consideration may be accepted by employees or members of their families from any supplier to McGraw-Hill."[7] It is impossible to read this statement in full and not be aware of McGraw-Hill's expectations about ethical conduct throughout the organization. Boards should approve, and in many cases take the initiative in developing, such policy statements.

---

[6]See for example the Ontario Mental Health Foundation's *A Plan for 1978-1983*, October 1977.

[7]*McGraw-Hill's Code of Ethics* (New York: McGraw-Hill, Inc.)

Another kind of policy statement refers to a specific issue and often arises from confrontation with a problem that has a satisfactory or unsatisfactory result. A corporation closes its plant in Winnipeg and expands its plant in Calgary. There are immediate critical responses by the union which was not consulted, by angry workers, and by disturbed citizens in Winnipeg. The media are very critical of the company. The result is that this whole problem is reviewed in detail by the board and a policy is developed in which, should a similar situation arise in the future, many of the unattended details and consultations required in such a move will be attended to. Or, as another example, a university board discovers many of its faculty are employed outside the university in activities unrelated to their academic duties. The board properly considers this matter and after consultation with the faculty association develops and implements a policy that restricts "outside-for-pay activities" in terms of time available and their relevance to academic work.

Frequently, when such problems arise, they are brushed aside or resolved on a quick *ad hoc* basis. But these problems provide opportunities for the board to explore situations more deeply and to develop policies that will provide important guidelines for the future. This is a board responsibility!

There appears to be, in the United States particularly, a trend toward using both inside and outside directors on committees which recommend to the board long-term goals for the corporation. Monarch Capital Corporation, a financial holding company with over $500 million dollars in assets, is in its third year of working with a formal long-range planning committee of the board. This committee is composed of four outside directors and two inside directors. The senior officer (CEO) is not a member of the committee but is occasionally invited as an observer or participant. The committee meets once a month and is responsible for development of the broad aspects of corporate long-range financial planning.[8]

While there are only a few examples of this practice in profit corporations, such committees are frequently used in non-profit corporations, some of which seem to lean heavily on the experience of outside directors.

2) *Financial Planning, Control, and Health:* Almost all directors recognize these as some of their major responsibilities. This may be less true in non-profit organizations but, as already stated, the obligation

---

[8]Mueller, *op cit.*, p. 48.

is no less and the need probably much greater. Consider this example: "J_____ L_____, former Chairman of the Laurentian Hospital Board in Sudbury, was jailed for six months yesterday for corruptly accepting secret benefits to rig bids to build the hospital."[9] One may well question the effectiveness of a board that would allow its chairman to deal unilaterally with contractors. Who is to say that non-profit boards have less responsibility than boards of profit corporations?

What is involved here are careful budget plans for capital and operating costs, financial arrangements for loans, the issuance of stocks and debentures—in short, a complete annual financial forecast. Once having approved a financial plan, the board has an obligation to assure itself in monthly reports that all is going as planned, and to take such steps as necessary to keep the corporation in a healthy financial position. A profit corporation, by its very nature, must take financial risks and not all such risks can be successful. The board's responsibility is to weigh these risks, ensure that an unsuccessful outcome will not ruin the company, make a decision regarding any available opportunities, and if the decision is positive, it must support management to the fullest extent possible.

Fiscal control and management often appear to be elements of operation which can be left to accountants and management. If this were so, we would not have witnessed the disastrous failure of the Penn State Railway, with its prestigious board; nor the Massey-Ferguson Board some years ago discovering, after the fact, that the Executive Committee (composed of Argus directors) had secured a large loan under conditions which could hardly be approved by a board who had all the stockholders' interests in mind.

This writer was a member of a board which was seriously concerned about the financial well-being of the company in spite of the fact that we were being presented each month with a financial statement that showed good bottom-line results. Three of the outside directors, who are by any count expert financial men, questioned the President and CEO at length about these statements without discovering errors of any kind. It was a minor incident which led to the gradual unravelling of extensive manipulations of financial data that had previously deceived us all. Several key persons including the President were immediately fired and new management hired. But what is important is that a board, whose membership included a number of sophisticated financial people, was unable to discover the

---

[9]"Ex-Boss of Hospital Jailed for 6 Months for Taking Bribes," *Toronto Star*, 1 February 1977, p. B2.

errors that were inherent in the financial report, for almost six months. In financial affairs vigilance is the word!

All this leads to the very great importance of the Audit Committee. By law, companies offering shares to the public must have an Audit Committee composed of at least three members of the board, the majority of whom must be "outside directors."[10] While the law is confined to these companies it is inconceivable that any corporation (profit or non-profit) of substantial size should not have an Audit Committee.

Audit Committees vary in the way they operate but their purpose is clear: to give the board, through a committee, an opportunity to examine in detail with the internal auditors and (separately if they choose) with the external auditors the financial affairs of the corporation. If the Audit Committee takes its work seriously it will insist that the external auditors be responsible to it (and not to management) and that a recommendation for the appointment of the auditors come from the Audit Committee rather than from management. While better sources of information may be considered, for the moment the best source for most corporations and their Audit Committees is the external auditor.

One tough member of an Audit Committee goes immediately to a review of expense accounts which he insists on examining at great length. His explanation: "If there is any monkey-business there, it is likely to be found in other parts of the operation as well." Each member may have a special clue or means for focusing on the mass of financial data presented, which are probably useful but no substitute for a detailed review of the whole financial picture.

Almost all large accounting and management firms have now produced literature on Audit Committees, so it is unnecessary to go into further detail here on how such committees function. Suffice to say that all corporations should now have Audit Committees and that each member of such a committee should have read one or more of the brochures available for the asking.[11] Any meetings of the Audit Committee—indeed of all board committees—should be open to all board members. The advantage of this practice, now found in several

---

[10]Section 165(2) states: "A corporation may apply to the Director for an order authorizing the corporation to dispense with an audit committee, and the Director may . . . permit the corporation to dispense with an audit committee on such reasonable conditions as he thinks fit." Thus some corporations may operate without an audit committee.

[11]See for example *The Effective Audit Committee* (Toronto: Clarkson Gordon & Company, 1977).

large U.S. corporations, is that it gives the new and/or conscientious director an opportunity to get detailed information and insight that would be impossible otherwise. There is a tendency among some directors to relax their own efforts in respect of financial statements because they believe they can rely on the work of the Audit Committee. Needless to say, the appointment of an Audit Committee—even a very effective audit committee—provides no grounds for non-members of this committee to be less vigilant than a "prudent person" should be.

As will be evident here and in later chapters, the importance of the external auditor is increased as he deals intimately and privately with the Audit Committee. The auditors themselves seem unenthusiastic about this greater responsibility. A 1978 report from "The Adams Committee" of the Canadian Institute of Chartered Accountants suggests that the Audit Committee, not the external accountants, are the responsible agents for identifying questionable corporate practices. As an editorial in the *Financial Post* says of this Report: ". . . the report devotes much space to explaining what an auditor cannot be expected to do. He can't be expected to detect fraud; he is not a detective—nor can he be expected to discover all errors or illegal acts; he is not a lawyer and can't sit in moral judgment on his clients. All he can be expected to do it seems is to conduct the audit according to generally accepted auditing standards—which might or might not uncover irregularities."[12] Such thinking is not consistent with that of many outside the "community of auditors." It is that very limited role that some auditors have defined for themselves which has permitted corporate fraud and unethical practice in the past. Certainly the corporate solicitor may need to be consulted by the Audit Committee on occasion, but the title of the *Financial Post*'s editorial is sound advice to members of an Audit Committee: "Don't let auditors off the hook."

3) *Appoint the Chief Executive Officer:* Many directors consider this their most important task; and with good reason. As one director said, "The better he is, the better we look". And, of course, few will question that it is the initiative, knowledge, experience, and motivation of the CEO that determines the character and success of the enterprise.

The cost of choosing the wrong CEO is immense. Henry Golightly estimates that it takes two or three years for a new president to demonstrate his lack of competence to the point where the board con-

---

[12]*The Financial Post,* 6 May 1978, p. 6.

cludes a "change must be made."[13] The cost of electing a CEO and terminating him in two or three years is impossible to quantify. "Interruptions in the pattern of revenue and income, and more important, the adverse impact on the morale and motivation of key people throughout the organization illustrate what can happen when the board fails to fulfill its roles and opportunities."[14]

This, then, is one of the major tasks of a board—to find the best person available for the position of CEO. Many believe that it is better to promote an insider rather than look for an outside executive. But circumstances differ. What seems essential is that the board have some means of evaluating the work of subordinates of the CEO and some knowledge of promising executives in other similar organizations. To avoid the trauma of change some corporations have established committees to study the problem of finding a successor to the CEO, so that if a change suddenly became necessary a well-informed opinion would be available.[15]

There are considerations beyond finding the right person. When a new CEO is to be appointed there is an opportunity to begin with a clean sheet, to irradicate dissatisfactions of the past, and to provide a fresh mandate for the CEO. What is most urgent, perhaps, is to clarify relations between the board and the CEO. This is the opportunity for mutual understanding—preferably put into writing—of precisely what duties are assigned to the CEO and what obligations the board has for monitoring the work of the CEO and the welfare of the whole enterprise. There are those who will argue that when one hires a competent person, one should give him a "free hand" to operate as he sees fit. However, a few years later this may be regretted. Indeed, there is much to be said for experienced directors keeping a tight rein on the new CEO until he has proven his or her capacity. In any case the appointment should be preceded by frank discussion about board-CEO relations, the kind of information the board will require, and the type of decisions it will insist on making.

The importance of a contract which details the conditions of employment has come to the fore through professional athletes and even through the conditions of association in marriage contracts. There should, of course, be a binding contract between the new CEO and the corporation. The contract should spell out the compensation in-

---

[13]Quoted in Myles Mace, "The Board and the New CEO," *Harvard Business Review*, March-April 1977, p. 17.

[14]Ibid, p. 30.

[15]Ibid, p. 31.

cluding salary, incentive bonuses, stock options, and benefits such as special pension provisions, house, car, etc.; it should specify if a term of office or tenure is involved; it should state under what conditions the CEO could be released and what compensation he could expect under such circumstances; it should indicate if after leaving the corporation the CEO is free to work for a competitor; it should state if there is to be a regular evaluation of the CEO's work and the manner in which the evaluation is to be carried out; it should indicate if the corporation is to carry insurance on the life of the CEO—to cover the cost to the corporation of finding a replacement.

There is, occasionally, an unpleasant obligation which rests with the board, i.e., to release or change the CEO. This a board does reluctantly, but when the need arises a strong board will take such action as did the Canadian Imperial Bank of Commerce Board when it accepted the resignation of its Chairman, or Union Gas whose board allowed its President to resign because of "differences of view and approach."[16] If the corporation requires a change of top management the board must see that this occurs. But there should be some compassion along with the firmness that is required to make such a decision. Many years ago I was director of a board which decided the CEO had to go. He was 62 years of age and the board made what we considered generous provisions for him: full salary until he was 65, after which he would receive a supplemented pension. Six months after he was released he died of a heart attack. Of course, he may have had such an attack under any circumstances, but that experience made us much more sensitive to what probably happens to a man's ego and dignity when he is fired or released. No amount of money will heal the hurt involved. There are now a number of reputable companies in what is called "the outplacement industry" or, as some say, "the firing trade."[17] Such companies have become skilled in helping boards plan and carry out an essential firing with a view to the welfare of the person involved, the company and its employees, and the public. The good board acts with strength, compassion, and skill in dealing with people.

---

[6]*The Financial Post*, 28 July 1979, p. 11.

[7]Judith Miller, "New Prestige for Those in Firing Trade," *New York Times*, 18 March 1979, p. F3.

Responsibilities of The Board

It may seem from the foregoing that a board has very great responsibilities; indeed that is true. But there are further obligations to which we now turn.

4) *Delegation of Duties:* A board must delegate certain duties to its CEO and often to committees such as finance, compensation, audit, executive, etc. Specific terms of reference are necessary for each. The precise terms vary from one corporation to another but an outline of what is delegated and expected usually can be found (or should be found) in the by-laws.

For example, a common statement in profit corporations is "subject to the Board of Directors the CEO shall have general control and management of the business and affairs of the company and the power to appoint and remove all persons other than those elected or appointed by the stockholders or the Board of Directors." In the case of a non-profit corporation, it may be stated as follows: "There shall be an Executive Director of the Hospital appointed by the Board who shall be the Chief Executive Officer of the Hospital and shall be responsible to the Board for the general administration, organization, and management of the Hospital including, but without restricting the generality of the foregoing, the employment, control, supervision and direction of all employees of the Hospital. He shall attend all meetings of the Board and of its committees without vote, and shall assure that the provisions of the Public Hospital Act and all regulations thereunder are complied with."[1]

The delegation of duties to the CEO varies little between profit and non-profit organizations but the idea seems to prevail that the latter is less accountable than the former. This may be because the non-profit CEO may be "an expert" (such as a doctor who is the head of a hospital or an academic who is a university president) in fields about which board members know very little. This should not be so, and board members of non-profit corporations have a responsibility to be suffi-

---

Sunnybrook Hospital Act of Incorporation and By-Laws, 1978, p. 11.

ciently knowledgeable that they can ask questions and make sound judgments about issues which come before them.

There is variation in the manner in which duty is delegated to committees. The by-laws of some corporations give considerable authority to committees, e.g.: "The Executive Committee shall have all the powers of the Board when the Board is not in session insofar as such powers can be legally conferred upon or delegated to the Executive Committee except in cases in which specific directions shall have been given by the Board."

In various ways, then, it would seem that the board can delegate to a considerable degree its responsibilities to a CEO and to its committees. But as Powell-Smith states: "Directors must *not* exercise their power of delegation so as to abdicate control of the company's affairs. It is therefore a breach of duty for the directors to appoint a manager with full powers to conduct the business free from any control and supervision. . . ."[2] And commenting on committees in both Britain and the United States, he states: "It is not unusual for an executive committee to be appointed to deal with matters arising between Board meetings, or a finance committee to be given authority to deal with financial matters. However, in appointing such committees, *the board is not allowed to abdicate authority and responsibility* or exclude minority representation and attempts by committees to usurp the entire control and management have been condemned in that country [U.S.A.][3] (italics mine).

There is an understandable tendency for the board to rely on the CEO and an established committee structure to do its work, but it must be emphasized again that ultimate authority and responsibility cannot be delegated. Thus, "under the Federal Act, while directors may delegate executive or administrative powers to a committee or a managing director, they cannot delegate their decision-making powers over the most significant aspects of corporate management on which shareholders are entitled to expect the considered attention of all directors."[4] It is probable that an increasing number of lawsuits in Canada will demonstrate this point.[5]

---

[2] Powell-Smith *op cit.*, p. 128.

[3] Ibid, p. 106.

[4] Jacobucci *et al, op cit.*, p. 280.

[5] See for example the judgment in the *Thorne, Riddell & Co.* case in which one of the defendants said: "We were entitled to rely on an agent but had to take full responsibility." "Judgment Places Greater Liability on Auditing Firms," *The Globe and Mail,* 6 June 1979, p. B1.

As indicated earlier, there are specific responsibilities spelled out in the Canada Business Corporations Act which clearly cannot be delegated by a board. These include (a) submitting to shareholders any matter requiring their approval, (b) filling a vacancy among the directors or in the office of the auditor, (c) issuing securities except in the manner and on the terms authorized by the directors, (d) declaring dividends, (e) requiring shares issued by the corporation, (f) paying a commission for sale of shares, (g) approving a take-over bid circular, (h) approving financial statement, and (i) adopting, amending, or repealing by-laws (Section 110-3).

There appears to be a tendency to use directors not merely to fulfill legal duties, but to organize committee work in a manner that will allow directors to focus on problems of greatest import to the corporation. In what is called a "significant breakthrough," General Electric (U.S.A.) in 1972 developed a new committee structure and assigned specific functions to five committees: operations; technology and science; public issues; management development and compensation; audit and finance.[6]

This represents a willingness on management's part to utilize directors' knowledge and experience in crucial areas of corporate activity. The committees do not, of course, usurp management's role but they do contribute to the formulation of policy and underline the importance of the board's function in establishing direction for the corporation.

5) *Monitor Progress:* There are two types of judgment to be made in respect of progress—quantitative and qualitative.

The quantitative judgments are easier to make. Assuming established goals re sales, expenses, income, etc., and assuming accurate reporting by management, a director should be able to assess whether the corporation is on course. Whether a profit or non-profit corporation, a careful examination of quantitative data should tell the director if, and where, problems exist and if it is time to raise a red flag. The alert director will not be deceived by a profit-and-loss statement that at first glance appears on target. He will want to know how the statement is affected by unanticipated price increases, inflation, foreign exchange, and interest rates, and whether unwise cuts in expenses have been made to improve the bottom line. Directors of non-profit corporations seem peculiarly inept in this respect. Whereas they would quickly identify financial trouble spots in a profit corpora-

---

[6]Mueller, *op cit.*, p. 47.

tion, in non-profit corporations they often seem to accept financial over-runs and deficits that have no justification. This is often because directors think they do not know enough to question the judgment of academics, doctors, artistic directors, or social workers. But in budget management they must. Courtney Brown states the trend when he speaks of hospital boards:

"The board should insist that senior members of the medical staff, heads of departments, chiefs of clinical services, and the chief of staff join with administrators in the preparation of overall budgets projecting both income and expenses. The rules of the hospital should stipulate, with medical staff concurrence, that expenditures for specific activities will be restricted to agreed allotments approved by the board. Budgeting, moreover, can help trustees to make more exacting performance requests of both medical and non-medical staffs. Indeed, it is desirable that the medical staff be adequately represented on the board, not so much as special pleaders for causes, but to assure that the medical staff is fully integrated into the overall conduct of the hospital. Transition from a system of dual control to one of integrated control through budgetary procedures is a complex task, probably involving many bruised sensibilities at first, but *it is essential if the geometric progression of hospital costs is to be restrained. Only the board of governors can make it happen*"[7] (italics mine).

The single most important goal for many CEOs in profit corporations is short-term profit maximization and for many in non-profit corporations the objective may seem to be a balanced budget—no deficit. The reason for this is primarily because a CEO is often judged by this criterion alone. Particularly if he can "turn a corporation around," that is, improve its financial position, his reputation is greatly enhanced. As a result, the CEO's vision is often narrow in scope and time.

This is a preface to saying the board must take a broad view, be concerned with long-term objectives and deeply interested in the morale and ethics of the organization and the quality of the product or service offered. It has a duty to make a profit and to balance a budget but, particularly in this era of changing attitudes, it has a further obligation to consider broad moral and social questions that hitherto could be largely ignored.

James Gavin, former chairman of Arthur D. Little, Inc., suggested that the tendency of some corporations toward isolation and withdrawal from global concerns, problems, and opportunities is, in the

---

[7]Courtney C. Brown, *Putting the Corporate Board to Work* (New York: Macmillan Publishing Co., Inc., 1976), pp. 137-138.

long run, the road to extinction for institutions.[8] The board, free from the pressures of everyday management, is in a position to put the business of the corporation in a wider context than the balance sheet. As one progressive director suggests: ". . . An individual who spends his or her life in the pursuit of greater corporate efficiency and maximizing the profits of shareholders is somewhat removed from the day to day ferment of political life".[9] Such a limited focus leads to the kind of isolation—and perhaps extinction—of which Gavin spoke.

Today there are new concerns about the environment, community improvement, health and safety, minority and female hiring and promotion, and even where to do business. These are broad issues which must gradually work their way onto board agendas.

This is far less esoteric than it may sound. The board represents the shareholders, the members, or the public, depending on the kind of corporation it is. But if the corporation is found to produce a poor product or service, to have acted unethically, ignored the interests of the community, treated its workers unfairly, etc., then in the long term the corporation may suffer in terms of smaller profits, or smaller grants, or decreased public support. It is in the interests of the corporation that the board be occupied with social issues and moral obligations. And a group of able citizens should be better able to make judgments in this area than a CEO, especially if he or she happens to be oriented to a single goal.

A careful study of the long drawn-out Inco layoffs and strike in 1979 is revealing in this respect. While the study does not allow the union, or the government, or the City of Sudbury to go blameless in the resulting ill-will which pervaded the whole incident, it implies severe criticism of the company for its handling of the situation. While, for example, Inco followed legal procedures in informing governments on the dates of layoffs, ". . . nothing was done to alert the Sudbury community in advance of the announcement about the scale of layoffs. As late as September 23 [the layoff announcement was October 20] some union leaders were even told Sudbury would be in a hiring position next January . . . one hour before the announcement [of the layoff] the mayor of Sudbury was informed."[10]

If we assume that Inco's image suffered greatly in this scenario (as seems to be the case), who in the organization is at fault? "The news

---

[8]Mueller, *op cit*, pp. 86-87.

[9]Brown, *op cit*, p. 7.

[10]"The Great Inco Layoff Dilemma," *The Financial Post*, 4 November 1978, pp. 40-41.

[of the production cutbacks and the reduction of about one-fifth of Inco's 21,500 person work force] came shortly after noon, October 20, following the Inco board meeting. . . .[11]" If the board was fully informed, if it was aware of all the implications of the proposed action, if it had reviewed the problem in its widest perspective, and had considered not simply the law and conventional business practice, but also the moral and ethical aspects of the problem, as should be the case,—if all these issues were present and considered at the October 20 board meeting and previous meetings and if the board approved the action taken—the result would seem to be the board's responsibility. And as this study indicates the timing of the announcement and the manner in which it was made, seem to leave a good deal to be desired. It may well explain, in part, why Inco was voted "the least popular of 100 organizations" by a sample of students of Ontario universities in 1979.[12]

6) *Make By-Laws:* Of all the duties of directors, the reading of the by-laws, one would judge, is the most neglected. And yet these, just as the law, govern the actions of the board. The by-laws, and any changes in them, must be approved by a meeting of shareholders or members, and since they guide the direction and manner in which the corporation operates, they are of the greatest importance.

In good part, the by-laws are of standard form and deal with such matters as the Annual Meeting and notices of when it is to be held, what constitutes a quorum, voting and conduct of the meeting; the board of directors, the number of directors, election of directors, directors' meetings, a quorum for such meetings, disclosure of interests, remuneration of directors, powers of directors, board committees and their terms of reference; officers of the corporation and their duties; stocks, loans, transfers, contracts, and undertakings; the protection of directors and officers; banking and banking procedures; the appointment of auditors. All of these by-laws to be stated in very general terms and allow for a good deal of flexibility in actual operation.

But there are differences between corporations such as the number of directors, the requirements for a quorum (and particularly under the new Canada Business Corporations Act for the number of Canadians required for a quorum both at directors' and committee meetings), voting rights, borrowing limits, signing officers, age of retire-

---

[11] Ibid, p. 40.

[12] "The Students Name Names," *The Financial Post,* 27 October 1979, p. 6.

ment of officers and directors; etc. A director should know the facts regarding the approved practices of the company of which he is a director and, particularly in this day, precisely what provisions are made for the indemnification of directors.

As already indicated, non-profit corporations often operate under a special Act and their by-laws reflect this fact. But directors or trustees have the same obligation to read and know the by-laws. One of the articles in the by-laws of a hospital states: "If, within any calendar year, a member of the Board, not having been granted leave of absence by the Board, attends less than 20 per cent of the meetings of the Board, he shall *ipso facto* vacate his office, and it is the duty of the Board, by resolution, to declare his membership vacant".[13] Unfortunately, "leave of absence" is too readily granted, but the requirement itself is sound and could well be included in the by-laws of profit corporations. Unfortunately there seems not to be disciplinary action for those directors who attend board meetings regularly but have never been heard to speak!

7) *Provide for Board Continuity:* One of the most important changes in board behaviour is the establishment of a nominating committee of the board to propose to the board a slate of directors for election at the annual meeting. The old practice of the CEO selecting a few "buddies" for his directors is clearly on its way out. Good riddance!

The task of the nominating committee is less easy than may appear. The practice has been to re-elect existing board members until they are required to retire at the age established in the by-laws. The latter was (and is) in many companies age 75 but the age of retirement for officers is increasingly becoming 65 and for directors 70. But the result of former practices is to have a board of older men who, unless for special reasons, cannot be replaced until their retirement age. There are several boards in which it is known that three-quarters of the members are over 65 years of age!

The wise nominating committee will know a spread of ages is essential for board continuity just as some spread in areas of specialization and competence is necessary for effective consideration of the many issues that come before a board. The committee will begin to collect names of "promising people" long before it is required to report. The list will include younger people of considerable potential, women and members of minority groups who have demonstrated competence, people who have "made it" and can be of value to the

---

[13]Sunnybrook Hospital Act of Incorporation and By-Laws, 1 January 1978, p. 4.

board, etc. The effort will be to build gradually a board of distinction in which no more than a third of the members will ever retire in a three-year period. To obtain this objective it may be necessary, as some corporations have done, to change the by-laws so that a larger number of directors can be appointed.

8) *Prepare Annual Report and Annual Meeting:* The traditional placidity of the annual meeting can no longer be guaranteed. As General Motors, Noranda, and dozens of profit companies, as well as non-profit corporations, such as the Ontario Art Gallery, the Social Planning Council of Toronto, etc., have discovered, the annual meeting may be a time of sharp questioning, criticism, and even confrontation by shareholders or members.

It is the duty of the directors to prepare an annual report and to plan the annual meeting. Of course, much of this work is delegated to auditors, solicitors, and officers of the company. But their work can no longer be rubber stamped. The audit committee and the board must be assured there are reliable figures; there should be disclosure of conflicts, of major policy decisions, of issues both present and anticipated. If this is to be the case the board must examine all aspects of a draft report carefully and prepare to deal with questions about decisions it has made.

At the annual meeting it was the custom for bank chairmen and presidents to comment on the nation's economy and economic policies—an effort to put the operation of the bank in a broad context. In the future we may well see not only banks but corporations of all kinds reporting not merely on the welfare of the corporations but on broader community and social issues with which it is inevitably involved.

Recently, a prominent socialist speaking to a large audience stated that "all the evidence suggests that corporations are much more interested in their balance sheets than the health and safety of their employees."[14]

In recent years most responsible companies have made mighty efforts to improve the health and safety of their employees. These efforts cannot be dismissed on the grounds that they are required by law or are "good business." Responsible companies are concerned about the welfare of their employees. But this concern is seldom revealed in annual reports or at annual meetings. The latter should be the locus not simply to report financial results, but also to explain ef-

---

[14]Stephen Lewis in a lecture at York University, June 4, 1979.

forts that are being made to deal with the many issues about which the public is interested. What is being suggested is not a propaganda blast but an honest attempt to explain the complexities of corporate life and the steps that have been taken to make the corporation a sound, progressive, humane, and purposeful organization.

9) *Give Impetus To Growth and/or Quality:* The traditional role of the board is to react to reports and issues raised by the CEO and, of course, it is the latter whose insight and initiative makes for expansion and higher quality. But board members themselves should be free to initiate ideas and proposals that might promote the purpose of the corporation. One thinks of three illustrations of this:

a) A board member suggested that the university of which he was a governor might invite the principals of neighbouring schools to a dinner for the purpose of encouraging enrolment, which was declining at the university. The university President thought it a good idea but not feasible financially. The board member took the initiative of inviting 100 principals to a private dinner which he paid for personally and at which the President spoke. The result was excellent.

b) A board member of a very successful company introduced the idea of expansion into a new field by purchasing a company that he knew (privately) the aging owners might be tempted to sell. There was some reluctance about such expansion ("don't move away from our expertise") but the director brought together the CEO and the aged owner at a lunch, a study was made, and a tentative plan developed which was, with little modification, approved by the board. The new acquisition has proven to be the most profitable division of the company during the past ten years.

c) A director with wide financial experience, believing interest rates to be on the rise, pressed the board and management to plan their financial affairs on the basis of this expectation. There was considerable reluctance, particularly on the part of the CEO, but gradually the director's views were accepted—and with considerable saving to the company.

All wisdom is not confined to corporate officers, nor do all ideas and actions have to originate with them. The board constitutes the senior layer of corporate structure and it should be as loyal and devoted to corporate objectives and policies as any other group in the corporation. The major role of the board may be advisory and disciplinary, but their contribution to the corporation can and should be much broader than that.

10) *Develop a Strong and Healthy Board:* This may be the place to em-

phasize several prejudices about that which helps boards become independent and strong.

While there is no data to support the assertion, it seems probable that a board functions more effectively if there are separate persons holding the position of Chairman and the position of CEO. If the CEO is Chairman, as he so often is, he plays a dual role, performing two quite different functions that are, in some respects, incompatible. The purpose of the Chairman is to introduce the issue, encourage discussion, summarize the points made, and secure agreement, if not concensus, on the resolution of the issue. The CEO should be free to participate in the discussion, to present data on the issue at hand, to reply to questions, to press his point of view. If the Chairman is the CEO, all discussion is focused on the chair; he reports, defines the issues, defends his position, and carries the burden of the meeting. This is not necessarily unworkable and confusing as some suggest,[15] but it probably centralizes authority to a greater extent than desirable in a good board. It puts the CEO in a position of defending a recommendation he has made, when as Chairman he should be encouraging the board to explore the problem in the widest possible terms. The point is that all other things being equal (i.e., the availability of a good Chairman *and* and a good CEO), a better board will result if these are two separate positions, held by two different people.

A good board is a disciplinary force in the organization. One director I observed for many years always had a question about one aspect of management's report. At each meeting he questioned a different part of the report and at each he pressed with follow-up questions until he was completely satisfied that management had the information and knowledge he sought. His explanation of this, when I asked him privately, was that a director could not cover all parts of management's activities at any one meeting, but by going into detail on one issue one could get a good idea if management had done their homework, were "on the ball," and were "on top of the job." Whatever else this practice did, it made management much more alert and better informed on all data presented to the board, for they never knew what issue would be raised or, as the CEO said, "where lightning would strike."

Another function performed by what might be called conscientious boards is that of self-examination, i.e., a close look at how they operate as responsible boards. This is not a common practice, but is nonetheless a commendable one and perhaps the only way change

---

[15]Courtney Brown, *op. cit.*, pp. 41-51.

can be induced. A sub-committee of Allied Chemicals composed of three outside members is charged to review "the general responsibilities of the board, its functions, talents, compensation and membership, as well as its organization, structure, size and composition, and then to advise and make recommendations to the full board on these matters."[16]

There are many other things that make for good board work: an efficient secretariat that handles the legal and clerical work; an agenda that separates routine and important issues; good relations between the board and the CEO; a diverse membership of mutual respect; stimulating board meetings in which there are new and interesting reports, issues, speakers and visits to various divisions of the organization; and an ethos of harmony and good will.

The ten items (listed in Chapters 5 and 6) by no means exhaust board responsibilities, but if these are fully met one can be certain that there is an able, conscientious, and well-motivated board.

---

[16]Courtney C. Brown, *op cit.*, p. 23.

Caveats—Why It Doesn't Work That Way!

The mythical conception of the profit corporation is one of a three-level structure with a limited democratic philosophy which spreads control and authority among the three parts of the organization. It assumes a large group of interested and informed shareholders who meet at least once a year to discuss the progress of the company, elect the board of directors, appoint auditors, and comment on corporate policy and progress, etc. It assumes a board, elected in open session by the shareholders, which has as members persons of independent spirit, competence, and concern for the interests of *all* shareholders. It assumes a management appointed by, and responsible to, the board of directors, who are servants of the company and obligated to follow the goals and policies adopted by the board and to report their activities in detail to the board. This is the model of the corporation as it may have been seen by those who studied and wrote corporate law and by those philosophers, economists, and citizens who believe in a free society in which there is decentralized power, open competition, checks and balances in the operation of private institutions. It is the model of the corporation we had in mind in discussing the legal and other responsibilities of directors in the previous chapters. Unfortunately this model does not apply in the real world as we know it today. In the next two chapters we will discuss why this is so.

II

The idea that every profit company has a huge number of shareholders is false. One thinks of Bell Canada or Consumers' Gas or the Steel Company of Canada each with thousands of shareholders, and, indeed, the shares of these companies are widely held. But these are not typical cases.

In a major study of shareholders of U.S. corporations,[1] it was found that most corporations have relatively few shareholders. A summary of this study suggests the following:[2]

---

[1] Melvin A. Eisenberg, *The Structure of the Corporation: A Legal Analysis* (Boston: Little, Brown & Co.), 1976, p. 42.

[2] *Ibid.*, p. 42.

Number of Shareholders	Approximate Number of Corporations
1-10	1,630,000
11-99	70,000
100-499	26,500*
500-1,499	5,000
1,500-2,999	1,700
3,000-10,000	1,200
Over 10,000	600

*This figure combines corporations with 100-299 shareholders (24,000) and corporations with 300-499 shareholders (2,500).

There is further evidence from a study by the U.S. Security Exchange Commission of the distribution of shareholders in an extensive sampling of over-the-counter corporations. This study showed the following:

a) in about half of the corporations with fewer than 1,000 shareholders, the ten largest shareholders held 50% or more of the stock,

b) in more than half of the corporations with 1,000 to 1,999 shareholders, the ten largest shareholders held 40% of the stock, and

c) in about half of the corporations with 2,000 to 4,999 shareholders, the ten largest shareholders held at least 30% of the stock.[3]

What do these figures mean? They suggest that relative to the number of corporations with shares on the market, there are very few companies in the United States in which the ownership is widely and evenly distributed to many shareholders—in which power is broadly spread over a large number of shareholders with little possibility of any one or two of these shareholders holding enough stock to control the corporation . . . or for an outsider to secure enough stock to manipulate a take-over without considerable stockholder participation.

On the other hand it means there are a very large number of companies with few (say under 5,000) shareholders and of these, it seems, about half are in the control of ten or fewer stockholders.

We have fewer studies of corporate ownership in Canada and less adequate data on which to clarify the position of the shareholder in Canadian corporations. A close examination of *The Financial Post*'s annual report of the largest industries in Canada is, however, revealing. The following table has been drawn from the data provided in this report:

---

[3]Ibid., p. 43.

Distribution of Ownership of *The Financial Post*'s 300 Largest
Canadian Industries (1979)*

Ownership	Ranking	Number of Companies			Totals***	
		1-100 Group	101-200 Group	201-300 Group		
100% owned by one shareholder		33	59	32	124 -	41%
Controlled by one or more persons**		53	41	62	156 -	52%
Widely distributed		14	2	4	20 -	7%
					300	100%

*Taken from data included in the listing of the 300 largest industrial companies (in terms of sales, earnings, and assets) in *The Financial Post 500*, Summer 1979.

**In law a corporation is a person.

***The ownership of one of these 300 companies is unknown; the total is therefore 299, but we have calculated percentages on the basis of 300.

Far from the popular conception that Canadian corporations have many shareholders whose votes (through proxies and at annual meetings) control the destiny and direction of the company, it can be seen that *only 20, or 7%, of the 300 largest industries in Canada are widely held*; by which is meant that no single individual or group has sufficient shares to control the company. On the other hand 123, or 41%, of these 300 industries have only one shareholder, i.e., they are completely owned by one person, family, group, or corporation. The public has no possibility of participation in ownership in these companies; except very indirectly in a few profit-crown corporations owned by governments or by owning shares (if they are available) in the parent company.

It will be seen that 156, or 52% of the corporations offer shares to the public but a "controlling interest" is held by one or more individuals or corporations. The degree of control varies from (say) companies like Canadian Admiral Corporation which is 99% owned by Rockwell International Corporation of Pittsburg to Massey-Ferguson Limited of which Hollinger-Argus Corporation owns only 16% of the shares. But even the latter is considered "closely held," as Hollinger-Argus (with its 16%, its contacts, and its supporters) is considered able to elect the directors and executive committee it wishes, and to control the direction of the company. Some of the companies in this category have a considerable number of shareholders (e.g., one company which is 86% owned by a U.S. corporation has over 5,000 Canadian shareholders) but in the crunch, when votes are counted, when power is to be exercised, it is the one or more large shareholder(s) who are able to decide policy, the directors to be elected, the dividends to be paid, the direction of the company. It could be said that a different picture or chart would appear if all corporations—and not simply the large industries—were considered. But a careful study of the 642 Canadian companies listed on the Toronto Stock Exchange[4] shows that:

a) 39% have fewer than 3,000 shareholders;
b) 70% have fewer than 6,000 shareholders.

Since these data exclude the many subsidiaries wholly owned by a parent company whose (subsidiary) stock is not for sale, and is therefore not listed on the Toronto Stock Exchange, the figures are the more startling. It can be said that (in spite of certain tax advantages on dividends for investors in Canadian companies) relatively few Canadians are shareholders and most of these buy or hold only a very small number of shares. To make the point another way—most Canadian profit corporations are wholly owned or closely held, and while a few of the latter may issue many shares, the large proportion of these are held by very few shareholders. Indeed, a study of those companies considered "the most widely held" in Canada indicates "that there has been a significant and large decrease over the last five years in the number of registered shareholders reported as owning shares of each company at its fiscal year end."[5]

The myth of a large spread of small shareholders controlling all our corporations is simply that—a myth. It does not exist in any but a very few companies in Canada. This is not to condemn the practice of single ownership or control but it is to state the fact that those who believe that small shareholders have any significant influence on the direction of Canadian industry simply do not understand how power operates in the modern world.

The law has moved, as pointed out earlier, to protect the rights of minority shareholders, and all corporations must be prepared to deal fairly and justly with these rights. Even a single shareholder can ap-

---

[4]Data compiled by author from figures supplied by the Toronto Stock Exchange.

[5]*Studies as to the Continuing Significance of Equities in the Canadian Market* (Toronto Stock Exchange, September 1976), pp. 3, 7, 8, 9.

pear and dissent or criticize in a manner that attracts media attention and embarrasses the company. Most corporations are becoming increasingly sensitive to such criticism.

But the reality is that there have been only a few lawsuits or overt protests by minority shareholders in Canada and corporations have means of dealing with all but a minority of these. Protests may be made and the corporation temporarily embarrassed but when the votes are counted—even with cumulative voting—the minority shareholder seldom wins. Most of those who hold a few shares in a company are primarily interested in the financial returns they receive and as long as these are adequate there is not likely to be any protest. If dividends or the stock price slips the tendency is to sell and buy into another company. The record is that few small shareholders have a vital interest in the direction and management of the company and that they will return their proxies as requested by management.[6]

III

We turn now to directors. Do they have the same kind of responsibilities and functions in these three types of companies (widely held, closely held, one shareholder owner)?

There is not only a difference of opinion about this question but also a difference in theory and in practice.

The problem is not for directors of widely held companies, for their duty in law and in public expectation is clearly to perform all of the duties outlined earlier; although it must be said that many of these companies are "management controlled" because of a lack of a skilled and/or responsible directorate and a lack of shareholder interest or action. Nonetheless, the nature of directors' duties is indisputable.

But for a subsidiary (of a parent company that owns or controls the subsidiary) there is considerable disagreement about the relative authority of the parent company vis-a-vis the subsidiary directorate. There are some who think the law leans in the direction of giving the parent company authority over the subsidiary and the latter's board of directors. For example, Chief Justice Traynor (Calif., U.S.A.) in a judgment (*Jones* v. *M. F. Ahmanson & Co.*) stated: "If a controlling in-

---

[6]The financial advisor of the *Toronto Star* replied to a query about a management proposal which would require a small shareholder to transfer his shares from voting to non-voting by saying: "The controlling group will presumably strengthen its hand but why make a fuss about it unless you have some tremendous alternative suggestions—you're going to get a dividend increase anyway—we're not in favor of power concentrations but *small investors have to be realistic*" (italics mine). Patrick Fellows in his column of 6 June 1979, p. B12.

terest (in one company is acquired by another) the acquired company will become a subsidiary of the acquiring [company] . . . and cease in fact, though not in law, to become an independent company. The parent company will wish to operate the subsidiary for the benefit of the group as a whole and not necessarily for the benefit of the subsidiary."[7]

This view is supported by the Canada Business Corporations Act in its interpretation of "unanimous shareholder agreement." It states: "An otherwise lawful written agreement among all the shareholders of a corporation—that restricts in whole or in part, the powers of the directors to manage the business and affairs of the corporation is valid" (140:2) and "a shareholder who is party to an unanimous shareholder agreement has all the rights, powers, and duties of a director of a corporation to which the agreement relates to the extent that the agreement restricts the discretion or powers of the directors to manage the business and affairs of the corporations, and the directors are thereby relieved of their duties and liabilities to the same extent" (140:4).

This judgment and these laws appear to be decisive and to allow parent companies to hold their subsidiaries and their directors in control. The "unanimous shareholder agreement" may provide directors of subsidiaries considerable freedom to "manage the business and affairs" of the subsidiary but it is clear that by "unanimous agreement" the shareholder(s) who owns all the shares of a subsidiary can invoke an agreement which would give him or her immediate and complete control of the subsidiary.

Most people in business would agree with this point of view. It is the parent whose long-term investment is involved and who would have to bear any major financial loss (particularly in the wholly owned subsidiary). Even "a controlling group" has interests and considerations that are beyond those of any one subsidiary, and these interests may require priority in any consideration of the subsidiary's plans. Therefore, it is generally accepted in business that directors of subsidiaries should defer to the wishes of the parent—indeed, as directors of a subsidiary that they have somewhat lesser obligations than they would have as directors of a parent company. This, in brief, is the case for parental authority.

But there is an opposing point of view—and not without some validity. For to accept the concept of limited responsibility or authority for directors of subsidiaries is to raise both the question of *limits* (what precise limits are placed on the duty and liabilities of the directors of a

[7] Eisenberg, *op. cit.*, p. 309.

subsidiary; where are these "limits" detailed; when and how are they subject to change; are such limits as exist in private or are they in the public domain?) and of *function* (what purposes are directors to serve if they have few significant duties to perform; are they merely "window dressing," status symbols for the subsidiary, advisors to the CEO who may or may not feel any obligation to follow the advice given?). These are difficult questions and no one can doubt they are confusing both to serious directors and to the public at large.

In spite of what has just been said about these questions there is some evidence in Canada to suggest that there are solid grounds for the hypothesis that directors of subsidiaries should accept far more responsibility than those who claim "our only responsibility is to the shareholder(s) who owns (or controls) this company."

In this respect the *Maple Leaf Mills* case (page 39) is instructive. It is almost inconceivable that the outside Canadian directors initiated the action to make Maple Leaf a 100% subsidiary of Norin. The scenario was probably one in which a decision to bring this about was made by Norin and its officers and the Canadian directors acquiesced or demurred or agreed, but finally approved the Norin proposal. Some directors would say that in any such situation it is the duty of the director to support and/or obey the parent's directive.

But when the court issued an injunction to prevent Maple Leaf from holding a meeting to approve the proposal, it said, in effect, that there were grounds to believe that the minority shareholder might have a case. And subsequently when this shareholder sued Maple Leaf, and each individual director for a total of $5 million, the responsibility of each director for the action taken came very much to the fore. The issue was settled out of court so we do not know which, if any, of the charges laid against the directors would be found valid. But the settlement itself was sufficient to indicate to some observers, at least, that the minority shareholder's case might have been heard with sympathy by the court. There is enough in this experience to indicate that directors of a subsidiary may be held liable for some actions of the subsidiary whether such actions are dictated by the parent or not. For some this is as it should be: directors are elected to perform certain functions and they should not hold office if they abdicate these responsibilities merely to carry out the wishes or demands of a parent company. Further support for this view is provided by a prominent Canadian legal authority who said: "Because of the power and position of management, it is sometimes thought that the outside director [in a closely held or wholly owned subsidiary] is powerless to take effectively any of the steps to which I have referred [i.e., the common responsibilities of all directors]. I disagree with this view. The *duties and responsibilities of such a director both in the legal and business sense are no different from those* [of directors of widely held corporations]. *The basis for fulfilling them is also in my view identical.* The difficulty, if it comes, may arise in actually carrying them out, for they may seem to run contrary to the desires of the parent. While it may seem easier to say than to do, I believe it is absolutely crucial that the outside director be prepared to put his directorship on the line where fulfillment of his duty is at stake"[8](italics mine).

Thus it would appear that apart from situations in which a parent corporation is able to exercise "unanimous shareholder agreement" to operate a subsidiary almost as it chooses, there are very solid grounds for holding to the view that directors of all companies should be prepared to carry out all of the duties we have outlined for them. In theory and, I believe, in law, this is the expectation.

But theory and law do not always govern practice. And while practice varies widely, it is on the whole contrary to the opinion expressed in the preceeding paragraph.

There are a number of parent companies which believe that authority should be decentralized and that each of their subsidiaries should have a good deal of autonomy to operate as they see fit. Thus, some directors will say that there is no difference between sitting on the board of a widely held or closely held corporation. This view, it seems, is somewhat naive.

There are at least four areas in which few parent companies, would provide complete autonomy. These are: (1) if the subsidiary experiences continuing losses, the parent may take action to alleviate this problem; (2) when the subsidiary prepares a long-term plan and set of objectives it is probable that the parent will want to study and alter and/or approve these; (3) when a new CEO is to be appointed the parent will want to be consulted and agree; (4) when major capital expenditures are anticipated the parent company will wish to review and approve or disapprove of these. (In actual practice most subsidiaries are given freedom to make capital expenditures only within strict limits established by the parent company.) At the very least, in situations such as the above, the parent will have a veto; on most occasions it will want to make the decision. Even in those subsidiaries in which a large degree of autonomy prevails, the parent company will insist on certain decisions or actions in special situations. Most boards of subsidiaries will accept such controls.

---

[8]R. C. Brown, "The legal responsibilities of a director" (Paper given at *The Financial Post* Conference, Fall 1978).

Seldom is there open conflict. The board of one company (which must be anonymous), proud of its autonomy even though wholly owned by a large U.S. corporation, voted to make a company donation to each of the two older political parties in Canada. The parent company objected. The Canadian board explained that while such donations might be illegal in the U.S., they were not only legal in Canada but were considered essential support for the democratic process. Further, it was a common practice in Canada, and most Canadian corporations made such donations. The parent company still demurred—it would embarrass them when their subsidiaries in other countries heard about the action of the Canadian board. It is difficult to assess the amount of pressure the parent company exerted, but it is probable that had the Canadian board not acquiesced by rescinding their decision, the parent company would have vetoed the action. But most subsidiary boards will understand and accept the reason and persuasion of the parent company.

We have been discussing subsidiary companies whose parent gives them considerable freedom. What of the others? Again there are no firm data to indicate what kinds of decisions parents allow their subsidiaries to make and which ones they reserve for themselves. The range is probably great but it is known that many parent companies, by using the "unanimous shareholder agreement" or simply by exerting their influence or authority, decide all major issues, allowing the subsidiary board to make only those decisions the law requires it to make.

In practice, therefore, subsidiaries have some minimal freedom, subject to the veto of the parent company; at a maximum subsidiaries have little, if any, freedom and are merely "rubber stamps" for the parent company. And since the board of a subsidiary or wholly owned company is elected by the parent the degree of control is further, if indirectly, exercised.

Thus, theory and law put aside, the boards of most large Canadian industries (93% of which are closely held or 100% owned) have some restrictions placed upon the responsibilities they should assume. It can be argued that this is as it should be, for it is the parent that is ultimately responsible for its subsidiary. However, I am only pointing out inconsistencies in theory and practice. Given the structure of Canadian corporations, it is not possible for many boards to carry out the duties the public expect them to perform. Crucial decisions are made by the parent company which carries the burden of responsibility for the well-being of its subsidiary.

Directors of subsidiaries may, of course, insist on assuming all the legal and moral obligations they believe to be theirs. If rejected or frustrated by parent directives, they can resign and make their reasons known publicly. Since most board members are prominent people the resignation of one or more directors is something most companies will do a good deal to avoid. Board members do, therefore, have a major card to play. It may well be that some stiffening of the spine and some willingness to face a confrontation on the part of some board members may lead to much more responsibility in the boardroom of subsidiary companies. As indicated earlier, there are some clues to suggest a gradual change in this direction may have begun.

Some distinction should be made between the company with one owner and those closely held. In the latter directors have a stronger base from which to operate as presumably some of the shares of the company are traded on the market. Such companies are subject to some degree of control by provincial securities commissions, which have been scrutinizing corporate operations with increasing care. Further, the directors are pledged to look after the interests of *all* shareholders alike, and not in any way to give privileges to major shareholders. The 1977 Ontario Securities Act makes this quite clear in respect of those who wish to purchase more than 20% of a corporation's stock: "He either goes to the open market and uses procedures intended to ensure an equitable deal for existing holders or he makes a tender offer to all holders of the voting securities—he doesn't strike a deal with a select few at a premium price and leave the minority holders out in the cold. . . . "[9]

While this deals with a special situation, the implication is clear—all shareholders must be treated fairly and equitably. Thus the board of directors in a company in which there is one or more large shareholder(s) need not be subservient to those who hold a majority or a "controlling" interest in the corporation. Realistically, one corporation (say Torstar Corporation) owning a controlling interest in another company (say Harlequin Enterprises) may need directors who will support Torstar's views when critical action must be taken. But some would claim that Torstar cannot act without regard for fair treatment and the welfare of Harlequin and its shareholders. To quote one legal opinion: "It would seem that the conclusion to be drawn from this case (*Scottish Co-operative Society* v. *Meyer*) is that where a subsidiary company is formed with an independent minority of shareholders, the parent company must, if it is engaged in the same class of business, accept, as a result of having formed the subsidiary, an obligation through its nominee directors to deal fairly with the subsid-

---

[9]"Protection for Minority Shareholders," *The Financial Post,* 16 April 1977, p. 4.

iary. If it fails to do so an action for oppression will lie."[10] It is clear from Lord Denning's judgment in this case that even directors appointed by Torstar to sit on Harlequin's board must deal fairly with Harlequin and its minority shareholders. It should not sacrifice Harlequin's well-being to satisfy a competing interest at Torstar. Inevitably there will be compromises, trade-offs, management decisions, but the directors of subsidiaries have clout and it would be encouraging to have them use it occasionally. They are not as impotent as they may think.

But as indicated there is considerable difference between what is and what should be. Certainly the myth that directors manage the business and affairs of Canadian corporations is, again, simply that—a myth. Most profit corporations are controlled or closely held by parent companies who restrict to a greater or lesser degree the freedom of directors of their subsidiaries. And, even in widely held corporations, the power of management, which often controls the proxy process, tends to subvert the authority of their boards.

IV

The third layer of corporate structure is that of management, appointed by and responsible to the board of directors. In the corporation that is wholly owned or closely held—the majority of large industries in Canada—the role of management is somewhat ambiguous. Since this role impinges in a significant way on the function of the board it deserves careful attention.

The trend in industry and commerce is not only toward multi-national companies but toward conglomerates, both of which may own or control hundreds of companies with total assets in billions of dollars. As an example we use the "Weston Empire" which controls Wittington Investments which in turn own 76% of Associate British Foods Limited and 56.8% of the George Weston Ltd. The latter has 53 subsidiary companies in Canada and the United States, one of which alone operates 500 supermarkets in North America and in 1978 had sales of $6 billion.[11]

In Canada there are perhaps a dozen such "empires", e.g., Canadian Pacific, Hollinger-Argus, Thompsons, Bronfmans, Power Corp., etc. It is not my purpose to argue for or against such conglomerates. On the positive side they are often able to provide the management skills and financial support that make it possible for some companies

---

[10]Powell-Smith, *op. cit.,* p. 119.

[11]*The Financial Post,* 7 April 1979, p. 21.

The Weston empire*

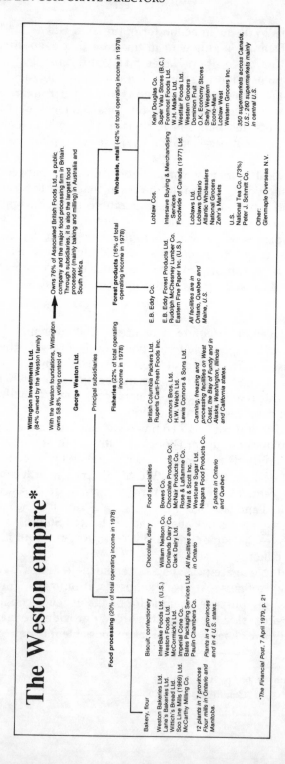

Wittington Investments Ltd.
(84% owned by the Weston family)

With the Weston foundations, Wittington owns 58.8% voting control of

George Weston Ltd.

Owns 76% of Associated British Foods Ltd., a public company and the major food processing firm in Britain. Through subsidiaries, it is also the largest food processor (mainly baking and milling) in Australia and South Africa.

Principal subsidiaries

Food processing (20% of total operating income in 1978)

Bakery, flour

Weston Bakeries Ltd.
Lane's Bakeries Ltd.
Wittich's Bread Ltd.
Soo Line Mills (1969) Ltd.
McCarthy Milling Co.

*12 plants in 7 provinces
Flour mills in Ontario and Manitoba.*

Biscuit, confectionery

InterBake Foods Ltd. (U.S.)
Weston Foods Ltd.
McCormick's Ltd.
Imperial Cone Co.
Bates Packaging Services Ltd.
Paulin Chambers Co.

Plants in 4 provinces and in 4 U.S. states.

Chocolate, dairy

William Neilson Co.
Donlands Dairy Co.
Clark Dairy Ltd.

All facilities are in Ontario

Food specialties

Bowes Co.
Chocolate Products Co.
McNair Products Co.
Rose & Laflamme Ltd.
Watt & Scott Inc.
Westcane Sugar Ltd.
Niagara Food Products Co.

5 plants in Ontario and Quebec

Fisheries (22% of total operating income in 1978)

British Columbia Packers Ltd.
Ruperts Carti-Fresh Foods Inc.

Connors Bros. Ltd.
H.W. Welch Ltd.
Lewis Connors & Sons Ltd.

Canning, freezing and processing facilities on West Coast, the Bay of Fundy and in Alaska, Washington, Illinois and California states.

Forest products (16% of total operating income in 1978)

E.B. Eddy Co.

E.B. Eddy Forest Products Ltd.
Rudolph McChesney Lumber Co.
Eastern Fine Paper Inc. (U.S.)

All facilities are in Ontario, Quebec and Maine, U.S.

Wholesale, retail (42% of total operating income in 1978)

Loblaw Cos.

Intersave Buying & Merchandising Services
Foodwide of Canada (1977) Ltd.

Loblaws Ltd.
Loblaws Ontario
Atlantic Wholesalers
National Grocers
Zehr's Markets

U.S.
National Tea Co. (73%)
Peter J. Schmitt Co.

Other:
Glenmaple Overseas N.V.

Kelly Douglas Co.
Super Valu Stores (B.C.)
Foremost Foods Ltd.
W.H. Malkin Ltd.
Westfair Foods Ltd.
Western Grocers
Dominion Fruit
O.K. Economy Stores
Shelly Western
Econo-Mart
Loblaw West
Western Grocers Inc.

350 supermarkets across Canada, U.S.: 260 supermarkets mainly in central U.S.

*The Financial Post, 7 April 1979, p. 21

to survive and prosper when they might otherwise fail. But their very size enables them to exert tremendous influence and their resources allow them to overwhelm competition and often to prevent the small independent entrepreneur from getting started or succeeding. An important question (to which we will return later) is whether directors of the parent company—the top group in the conglomerate—do not have some higher responsibility than the average director and do not require on their boards broader representation than do boards of less size and influence. A good case can be made for requiring these vast empires to be governed by a board representing a variety of public concerns.

For the moment, however, we are concerned with the management of subsidiaries. At best management in such companies has divided loyalty: (1) to its board of directors and (2) to its parent company. But for the CEO and perhaps his colleagues as well, the prior loyalty probably is to the parent company. The reason for this is that the CEO sees his status, his promotability, his future in terms of judgments made by the parent company rather than his own board of directors. It is often how the parent company evaluates his work that determines his salary, his chances for promotion, his opportunity to move to a higher rank in the empire. He must, of course, have good relations with his board (which in any case probably are members of or close to the parent company), but it is the senior officers of the parent that are often seen as the real determiners of his future.

Further, the relation of the parent company to its subsidiary is often on a management-to-management basis. The owner or CEO of the parent company (or one of the many specialists in his office) relates directly with the CEO of the subsidiary. While this relationship may be largely confined to management decisions, there is little question that many times important policy decisions are also made.

Both of these realities (loyalty to the parent company and management relations) tend to depreciate or by-pass the legitimate role of the board of directors of subsidiaries. They destroy or tend to destroy the role of the board as the authority to which management must be responsible. Thus again the reality is far from the ideal. The mythical model of the three-level concept of governance of the modern Canadian corporation is not fully applicable at any of the three levels.

In some respects and in some situations the problem in crown corporations, hospitals, and universities is similar. If the chairman of a crown corporation assumes his principal relationship is with the ministry that has established the corporation; if the CEO of a hospital believes his major contact is the government department of health that provides his hospital with funds or with the provincial or federal hospital association that has political clout; if the president of the university sees the government or the provincial advisory council on universities as the principle determinant of his university's future; etc.—in all these situations the authority of the board is considerably diminished. The myth is that the board manages and directs; the reality for these corporations is that money and power come from the government. The growing presence of the latter in many non-profit corporations radically alters the inner constitutional structure of these corporations.

V

There is one other development that requires attention because of its impact on corporate governance and policy. This is the emergence of "the money managers" as major investors who watch company developments with great care.

The largest of these are the pension fund managers but there are portfolio managers of trust, mutual fund, life insurance monies as well as corporations and individuals with large amounts of money to invest. It is estimated that there are more than $60 billion in pension funds in Canada ($30 billion in private employer-based plans and the rest in Canada and Quebec pension funds, registered retirement savings plans, civil service plans, etc.).[12] Where an ordinary individual may purchase 100 or 1,000 shares of stock, "the money managers" may purchase one million or more shares. They have become the big financial men.

The importance of this for us here is the influence of these managers on company operations. For example, Company A seeks to take over Company B. It offers $30 for the stock of Company B which on the current market is valued at about $24. The board of directors of Company B decides this offer is insufficient and not in the best interests of the company. But its largest shareholder is a pension fund, the manager of which says, "If you run a pension fund and somebody is offering $30 for a $24 stock it's almost a breach of fiduciary duty not to take the $6 gain."[13] He exerts great pressure on the board of Company B and its judgment can be influenced, if not determined, by a very large shareholder who has responsibilities other than the welfare of Company B.

---

[12]Jack McArthur, "There's 60 Billion in Pension Fund Clout," *Toronto Star,* 9 December 1978, p. B7; see also "Big Investors on Edge," *The Financial Post,* 24 March 1979, p. 1.

[13]"Takeovers," *The Financial Post,* 31 March 1979, p. 1.

And as the opportunities for sound investment in Canada appear to decline,[14] the money managers are being forced to look carefully at the policies of companies in which they have huge investments. Hitherto if the company did not do well, the tendency was to sell out and invest in another company. But there are fewer such opportunities now, and while it is far from common practice "the money managers" may begin to put pressure on boards and CEOs to move in certain directions—to begin to interfere with the functions of the board. It is almost certain such practice will become more prevalent in the future. Peter Drucker has suggested that employee pension plans would own more than 50% of the equity in U.S. business by the mid-1980s.[15] It is not inconceivable that managers of these funds may wish representation on the boards of companies in which they invest or that they will attempt either directly or indirectly to influence board policy.

Especially cogent is the potential of trade unions with many members and large pension funds to desire or demand certain business practices. A haunting question is whether these workers will, like students in universities, insist their pension fund managers invest only in companies that meet their criteria of "good companies." Some Canadian businessmen consider such action "pretty remote." It may be useful to describe the activities of the Amalgamated Clothing and Textile Workers in respect to J. P. Stevens & Co. in 1979.

Stevens & Co. was the second largest U.S. textile manufacturer which fought off unionization for over 16 years. The ACTWU began a campaign to isolate Stevens and to alienate and polarize the corporate and Wall Street communities away from J. P. Stevens.

"Last winter the ACTWU organized a campaign that led labor unions to threaten to withdraw more than $1 billion in pension and other funds from New York's Manufacturers Hanover Bank unless it dumped two of its directors, who also held seats on the Stevens board. The bank quickly caved in and failed to renominate Stevens Chairman James D. Finley and David W. Mitchell, chairman of Avon Products. Two weeks later Mitchell, deluged with letters from union sympathizers threatening a boycott of Avon goods, also quit as a Stevens director.

"Next the ACTWU turned its ire on the New York Life Insurance Co. by announcing that it would run its own candidates for the board

---

[14]"Big Investors on Edge," *The Financial Post,* 24 March 1979, p. 1.

[15]Jack McArthur, "There's 60 Billion in Pension Fund Clout," *Toronto Star,* 9 December 1978, p. B7.

against Finley and New York Life's chairman R. Manning Brown Jr. A contested election would have cost the insurance firm as much as $6 million to mail ballots to its policyholders, and New York Life decided that it was not worth the fight. Stevens' Finley was again knocked off a board—this time New York Life's—and he was furious. Meanwhile, Brown, who had earlier vowed not to give in, resigned from the Stevens board. Said he: 'I must consider the interests of New York Life.'

"But that was only the beginning. Now the union is going after E. Virgil Conway, chairman of the Seamen's Bank for Savings in New York City, who refuses to quit as a director of Stevens. The union is stirring up activist groups against Seamen's by pointing out that the bank makes most of its mortgage loans to borrowers outside metropolitan New York. The ACTWU has also enlisted political, labor and religious groups to help block the bank from opening a branch on Long Island."[16]

The above may be a relatively isolated incident but if it is successful, as it promises to be, the practice may spread, as it has among students who pressured their university boards to redraw investments from companies whose policies are in conflict with those of a part of the student body.

Thus, directors are likely to be confronted with many difficulties in the future. If conglomerates continue to increase and/or expand in the future, directors of subsidiaries who have been used mainly for prestige or for advice may find themselves in conflict with a law and a public expectation that will be more demanding than in the past. Withal there may be increasing pressure from parent companies, money managers, union pension fund personnel. For the serious and sincere director it will not be a life of leisure.

---

[16]"New Weapon for Bashing Bosses," *Time*, 23 July 1979, p. 35.

Other Blocks To Good Board Performance

Many directors now seem conscious of increased responsibilities in their role as board members. But change in the ethos of the boardroom is not easy to make. Indeed, the conscientious reformer sometimes appears like Sisyphus pushing a rock up a hill. There are numerous reasons for this, and some of these will be discussed briefly in this chapter.

II

Perhaps the most important block to effective board work is that of the power structure of each board. It is most obvious where there is external control as indicated in Chapter 7. Henry Ford is reported to have said to a fellow member at a board meeting of Ford: "Let's go and play golf Harry; we'll probably change everything they decide anyway." There are few such overt exercises of power today but the subtle influence of a parent company is sometimes as perverse.

But there are many other kinds of power which affect board activities. There is the place of key committees, particularly the Executive Committee. The few individuals on this Committee often become powerful in the sense that they become intimately acquainted with the operations of the corporation, become far more knowledgeable about the company or the hospital or the university, and it is often considered neither polite nor sagacious to question the judgment of these individuals—particularly if their report is brief and authoritative. It is easier to take issue with management than with a fellow director. Similarly other committees with special assignments may have unusual authority. The reports of these committees may well restrict rather than encourage discussion.

There is also on many boards "a power figure" who by virtue of wealth or experience or knowledge has special status. Board members are often reluctant to challenge such a person's judgment. There is such a person on one board on which I sit. He is an older man of great prestige who seldom speaks but when he does it is in the voice of authority—a judge handing down a sentence—and no one on that board has to my knowledge ever questioned his conclusions.

Further there are persons with special knowledge or skill who can dominate and inhibit discussion on certain issues. The CEO can speak dogmatically about certain internal developments, the solicitor speaks with authority about the law, the doctor about medical equipment, the academic about research. The average layman is hardly in a position to challenge statements from such persons and even his questions, difficult to formulate in any case, are sometimes treated with little tolerance.

All boards have power figures, either those referred to above or people who have great capacity to articulate their views, and all in one way or another prevent the board from functioning as a group of equals interested in pursuing every important issue to the point that it is clear, understood, and agreed upon by all.

III

Every board has its own distinctive character. It has (usually) a distinctive ethos; its own configuration of members, place and time of meeting, seating arrangements, agenda, method of doing its business, and provision for social occasions such as lunch after its meeting. What happens is that these practices become deeply embedded in the life of the board—as the social scientists says, they become institutionalized—and they are extremely difficult to change.

The advice usually given to a new director is to be quiet and watch for a few meetings and "you will see how things are done." The effect is to retain the *status quo* and discourage any desire for change. It is very difficult, as anyone who has made the effort knows, to break the hard crust of custom. Early in my career I was bold enough to make a suggestion for a change in practice at one of the first board meetings I attended. The Chairman looked at me, raised an eyebrow in obvious disdain, said "thank you for your suggestion," and proceeded with the regular business of the meeting. I learned that change does not come so easily nor in that manner.

The surprising aspect of this is that there is seldom significant change even when a new CEO and/or chairman is appointed. It is a time for change, for experimentation, for "a new deal." But as those who have observed a change of leadership know, bright new ideas or methods that may appear are either passed over or are co-opted into existing practice, and the life of the board goes on as usual. In a board that needs to change to meet new responsibilities "the institutionalization of practice" is a very considerable block.

IV

The conception of his role plays an important part in how the director performs on a board. Unfortunately, many directors of both profit and non-profit organizations hold traditional views about this role. These views assume that the director's role is not a time-consuming one—how else to explain the behaviour of very busy executives who sit on the boards of five to ten outside profit companies, *and* on the board of a hospital, *and* on the board of a university? Obviously such a person can give only limited time to each. As an examination of board memberships will show, this is not an uncommon practice.[1] It suggests that not only the individual director but the corporation itself does not expect that membership on the board will be time consuming.

There is very little question that the limited time given to any one of these enterprises can be, and often is, of very great value, for those giving even limited time are, on the whole, knowledgeable, experienced, and highly competent people. An hour's discussion with one of them may be far more useful than ten hours with less knowledgeable people. But an hour or two a month is not sufficient time to know the organization well enough to make the kind of decisions that the law and society require today. True, these people of experience can often spot a potential problem long before less experienced people would see it, as was the case when some members of the board of Canadian Imperial Bank of Commerce challenged the activities of its highly prestigious Chairman. But as evidence mounts (particularly through exposure of the activities of many U.S. corporations) that many boards have little knowledge of what goes on in the organizations they are supposed to manage or to monitor, it is increasingly clear that responsible people must limit the number of outside organizations for which they are individually and jointly responsible as members of the board.

The old pattern, however, seems to persist in many Canadian corporations. There is the assumption that the board has limited legal and advisory functions, that the principal value of board membership is that it provides social and business contacts, that one must maintain harmonious relations with other board members and therefore criticisms of any actions must be muted, and, if one has confidence in the CEO, all will be well.

Indifference to one's obligations as a director can go to extremes. A

---

[1] Peter C. Newman, *The Canadian Establishment*, vol. 1 (Toronto: McClelland and Stewart, 1975), pp. 38, 64, 106-7, 406-14, etc.

question in the Ontario Legislature asked if E. P. Taylor and the directors of Canadian Breweries should not be prosecuted for their failure to hold annual meetings of Peller Brewing Co., a company "controlled" by Canadian Breweries. The question was by-passed in the Legislature on procedural grounds, but "a few weeks later Peller's Brewery held their first annual meeting in 14 years. In fact, they held 15 annual meetings that same afternoon to cover all the annual meetings missed back to 1954."[2]

As indicated, these ideas and practices continue in Canada. While there are signs of change in the attitude of board members[3] these attitudes have, on the whole, yet to be translated into action. One will find among many young directors an aggressive attitude that suggests that change is taking place rapidly. But the evidence that we have indicates that there has not been significant change in the majority of Canadian boardrooms.

In the United States, Congress and the Security and Exchange Commission have fixed boards of directors as the ultimate overseers of corporate morality and the legal guarantors of the accuracy of information given to stockholders in prospectuses, earning statements, and disclosure notices of mergers, acquisitions, and divestitures. "To run afoul of the SEC in these or any other of a host of other areas is to invite class action suits."[4] The result is that many directors of U.S. corporations now give detailed attention to their duties. One head of a multinational corporation describes his work as an outside director of another company: "I'm spending two and a half days a month on board related homework. You wouldn't believe the material I have to go over just to keep a working knowledge of the company, its problems, its competition."[5] Until Canadian directors see their responsibilities in similar terms, it is unlikely they can bring to the boardroom the kind of informed judgment that will make board meetings meaningful and vital.

As pointed out earlier (although we have no data to support the view), it seems possible that some directors of major non-profit organizations take their responsibilities more seriously and give far more time to these organizations than they do to profit corporations. Why this is so is uncertain. Undoubtedly, one factor is that the chairman is an outsider who is a volunteer. The tradition in some old established

---

[2]"The Not-So-Secret Life of an MPP," *The Financial Post*, 24 March 1979, p. 6.

[3]Peterson, *op. cit.*

[4]*Wall Street Journal*, 8 October 1979, p. 24.

[5]Ibid.

non-profit organizations, particularly hospitals and universities, is that the lay chairman accepts a heavy obligation and time commitment, and that as chairman he must demonstrate leadership and initiative.[6] He sets an example that other board members often emulate. In profit organizations the tradition seems to be that initiative and leadership come solely from the CEO.

V

Another block to effective board operations is the view of many directors that one mustn't "cause ripples," that is, cause difficulty, embarrassment, or lack of harmony at board meetings. This philosophy is that of Sam Rayburn. "If you want to get along; go along." Any close observer of board meetings will see this philosophy in action. At one non-profit corporation board meeting, the finance committee brought in a completely inadequate report—a one-sheet forecast for the year ahead which indicated a million dollar deficit—which the board was asked to approve. It was clear by the questions raised that many members of the board were unhappy with the lack of detailed information and with the prospect of a deficit of this magnitude. But the Chairman of the Board and the Chairman of the Finance Committee both made it clear that they had examined the situation in detail, and the implication was that to vote against such a budget would be tantamount to a vote of non-confidence in them. Needless to say the underlying dissent was kept under control, discussion ceased, and the budget was passed. In most boards, members feel they must "go along" even though they believe, as in the case above, the action proposed is improper or unwise.

VI

A devastating handicap to any board is the lack of adequate information about the inner workings of an organization and the real issues it faces. One of the advantages that a board of a recognized hospital has is a careful survey by a group of outside specialists who examine and report in some detail on policies and practices in the hospital, before deciding to grant, or not to grant, accreditation to the hospital. Inevitably such a survey reveals matters about which the board was ignorant. It would be useful if all profit and non-profit organizations had such surveys and the boards had access to their results.

---

[6] See, for example, the initiative shown by Sir Joseph Flavelle at the Toronto General Hospital and the drafting of the 1906 University of Toronto Act in Michael Bliss, *A Canadian Millionaire* (Toronto: Macmillan, 1978).

There is perhaps a natural tendency for CEOs not to burden the board with mountains of data and to be selective in what information they present to the board. It is perhaps natural also that they select "good news" for board members and that some difficulties or problems are left out of their reports.

No board can operate effectively unless it has the vital information necessary to understand the corporation and the issues it faces. A lack of a steady flow of information to board members inhibits their performance.

VII

A further block to satisfactory board work is the lack of adequate control techniques, especially in financial areas. Most boards, with justification, accept at face value the reports of the financial officers of the corporation, of the external auditors, and of the audit committee; "with justification," because on the whole these are honest and competent people. But there have been a sufficient number of disclosures in recent years to alert boards that financial reports must be scrutinized with care. It is not adequate for the audit committee to meet once a year or to accept without question the auditor's or solicitor's report.

An interesting court decision in Quebec in 1979 gives emphasis to this point. In preparing a financial statement for a prospectus to be issued by Pan American Cruises Ltd., the Canadian auditors (Thorne Riddell & Co.) relied, in part, on a report of a U.S. firm that had audited the balance sheet of Pan American's U.S. mining subsidiary. This latter report was found in some instances to be inaccurate. Some stockholders sued the Canadian auditors and were awarded damages totalling $142,000. The plaintiffs also sued the legal firm that drew up the prospectus, but this action failed.[7]

Mr. Justice Nolan in his judgment stated: "When the auditor prepares a balance sheet which he knows is going to be inserted in a company prospectus offering a stock for sale I believe he has a duty to make sure that the contents of the balance sheet are accurate so that the prospective investors will not be led into error by it."[8]

This would seem to place heavier responsibilities on auditors and to lessen the burden of the board about the accuracy of financial statements. And while the action against the law firm failed, it seems reasonable to suppose that in other circumstances such firms would

---

[7] "Judgment Places Greater Liability on Auditing Firms," *The Globe and Mail*, 6 June 1979, p. B1.

[8] Ibid.

have similar responsibilities to those placed on auditors. Since no corporation wants to be involved, even though indirectly, in a court case of this kind, it behooves the board to question its auditors and lawyers at length.

But also of importance may be the implication in this judgment that just as accountants and law firms may be held accountable for accepting at face value the report of "experts," directors may now be questioned about their ready acceptance of the reports of "the experts" they depend upon.

VIII

We have already commented on the role of the chairman and the desirability of separating the office of chairman and the CEO. Whether this is done or not, the manner in which the chairman functions is critical to the way the board operates. I sat on one board where the Chairman seemed obsessed with getting the meeting finished on time. He was proud of the fact that one meeting had lasted only half an hour and he appeared ever eager to break this record. This, of course, is an extreme case of poor management but it must be said that there are not many skilful chairmen and the lack of these skills tends to prevent a board functioning as well as it might. The chairman's role in preparing the agenda, speeding through routine items, providing the kind of information required to deal with major issues without at any time seeming to rush or inhibit discussion, and his skill in summarizing and bringing together varied threads of discussion are all crucial, along with other capabilities, to good board meetings. Unfortunately, these skills are found infrequently.

IX

Of crucial importance is the attitude of the CEO. If his loyalties are divided, as indicated in the last chapter, he may see his board as a liability or at best a necessary evil. If his attitude to the board is negative or neutral he has many ways of preventing the board from performing as effectively as it should. One CEO is reported to have said, "You treat the board like mushrooms—keep them in the dark and feed them a little manure now and then" and another commented that "the only thing worse than a director who does not do anything is one that does." These probably do not represent the views of many CEOs, but the fact that they are often quoted with amusement is in itself significant.

The CEO can be a considerable block to good board work or, equally, he can be a most important factor in providing the atmosphere, information, issues, and challenges that make the boardroom alive and vital.

That CEOs can change in this respect is illustrated by the experience of one board which sent three of its members to meet with the CEO, to express dissatisfaction with his attitude to the board, the information he provided, etc. The CEO rose to this challenge and there was a dramatic change in the quality of directors' meetings. Perhaps this sensible method of dealing with such a problem could be tried in many corporations. The CEO may simply be following or doing what he thinks is expected of him—and this may be to follow the routine of the past.

X

Finally, boards themselves often unconsciously block effective work by their ignorance of how to go about improving or changing present practices. If they were deeply concerned about their work, boards would subject themselves to outside consultants who would appraise the quality of their meetings; they would constantly seek out fresh and vigorous views to enliven board meetings; they would ask penetrating questions and not be satisfied with perfunctory replies.

In short, those boards that do not operate the way they should are blocked from doing so for a wide variety of reasons: lethargy, subservience to a parent company, inadequate information, a non-supportive CEO, an unskilled chairman, a commitment to tradition and the status quo, a lack of knowledge of their duties, and so forth. All these factors block board productivity.

Three Models For The Reform of Boards

There have been many suggestions for the reform of boards of directors practices but few are sufficiently comprehensive to warrant close scrutiny. In the late 1970s however there began to appear thoughtful studies of the whole board process. I have selected three of these to summarize and illustrate rather different ways of approaching board reform. While I do not endorse fully any one of the proposals made, all are serious and illuminating studies of the problem and are worthy of careful consideration.

II

The Royal Commission on Corporate Concentration[1] gave considerable attention to the question of corporate ownership, control, and management. There is therefore a major section of the Report that deals with the role of directors.

The Commission is firm in its belief that this is a new era for boards of directors and that the latter must respond to this challenge. This is because (a) people are becoming more aware of the impact that corporations have on their lives and will insist that corporations be more responsive to public needs; (b) the corporate image is seen in an unfavourable light and the board, being composed of visible people could do much to improve the corporate status; (c) boards have been neglectful of their legal duties and should become aware of new obligations placed upon them by law; and (d) management should recognize that more of the burdens of directing the corporation should be shared with directors.[2]

The Commission makes a brave, if somewhat confusing, attempt to separate the role of the CEO and that of the board. It is less successful in making this distinction than in expressing its view of the duties of directors. It is worth noting however the sections below, particularly those in italics:

---

[1] *Report of the Royal Commission on Corporate Concentration* (Ottawa: Ministry of Supply and Services Canada, March 1978).

[2] Ibid., pp. 293-294.

95

"The Commission thinks that the board should not be expected to duplicate the role of the officers of the corporation: the board is not intended or designed to be, and should not try to be, a second level of management. But that does not mean that the board should be totally divorced from the function of management, or totally dependent on management for information. *Directors are given the right and the responsibility of managing the business of the corporation, and, by practice and convention, this means directing the management of the corporation's business.* To fulfill this obligation adequately, directors must be sufficiently knowledgeable about the corporation's affairs to ask management the right questions, and to be able to judge whether or not they are receiving the right answers. The role of the board should include the initiation of and participation in active discussion on issues of corporate policy (especially those that might reasonably be expected to come under some later public scrutiny). *The role of the individual director should also include the initiation of and participation in such discussion, even though that may appear unsettling and unnecessary to management.*

"*In short we see an expanded role for directors.* Directors must monitor management: this is their duty in the interests of the corporation, and it will be in the best interests of all affected by the corporation. *The responsibility flowing from the proper exercise of this function will require directors to spend more time on the affairs of the corporation than they normally do now.* To advance the concerns of the corporation (and its shareholders) in a manner consistent with the interests of the community in which it functions, *directors will have to be concerned with, and cognizant of, matters beyond those brought to the board's attention by management. The board should act as a check on the executive, be fully informed of the company's affairs, and be able to monitor the actions of management.* Any other role for directors will be inadequate and will result in their being the "captives" of the management that selects them"[3] (italics mine).

The Commission makes four major recommendations and a number of others related to board and corporate operations. Of first importance are the following:

1) *Boards and some committees should be composed largely of persons from outside the company.* By "outside," the Commission means persons who are not present or former officers of the company; who "do not have a close contractual or advisory relationship with the company (including parent and affiliates) or management such as would be the case with the company's outside counsel or its underwriter."[4] It is

---

[3]Ibid., p. 294.

[4]Ibid., p. 294.

recognized that the latter can make a valuable contribution and the Commission is not insistent but concedes: "Where a substantial proportion of the directors are truly outsiders, there need be less concern over the presence of a director who is also in a professional relationship with the company."[5] But the burden of the recommendation is to free board membership from those who, by virtue of present or former obligations, cannot be independent of management.

Again, however, there is a *caveat:* in cases of wholly owned small subsidiaries which are in effect divisions of the parent company, it accepts as fact that "boards of directors are little more than a formality."[6] But in larger and foreign-owned subsidiaries "we think . . . such boards should have outside members for the same reasons that apply to other large corporations."[7] The Commission does not state what a large or sizeable corporation is.

2) *Individuals should not sit on the boards of more than a very few publicly held companies.* If duties of the directors are to be expanded as the Commission recommends (and as stated above) a person cannot give the time required to any but a small number of boards.

3) *The audit committee should have increased responsibilities.* This committee should be the financial watchdog, particularly "in connection with transactions involving potential conflict of interests among directors, officers, major shareholders and the company."[8]

4) *Directors should increase their direct contact with the company's outside auditors and its outside counsel.* The purpose of this, of course, is to encourage directors to obtain additional information, advice, and clarification about corporate activities so that directors can make wise decisions. This adds weight to the argument (in 2) that the new role of the director is a time-consuming one.

While not making a specific recommendation, the Commission makes a good case for diversification of board membership, i.e., members drawn from a fairly wide cross-section of the public to end the virtual monopoly of businessmen as board members. "More Directors with the necessary intelligence and good judgment could be found among those who have had experience elsewhere than in business."[9]

---

[5]Ibid., pp. 295-296.

[6]Ibid., pp. 295-296.

[7]Ibid., pp. 295-296.

[8]Ibid., p. 296.

[9]Ibid., p. 297.

These constitute the major recommendations of the Commission. There is discussion of public directors, worker directors, and interlocking directors. About the first two it shows little enthusiasm and about the third its research suggests no present dangers.

The Commission has a good deal to say about the proxy machinery and urges: (a) much more relevant and important information be provided in the proxy information for shareholders; and (b) that boards have nominating committees composed of outside board members, in other words, to take appointment to boards out of the hands of management and to provide some degree of independence (from management) for new board members.

There is a section on "conflicts-of-interests" but this does not go beyond the conventional wisdom that board members must not only refrain from voting on issues in which they have a material interest but be particularly careful of all dealings with the corporation if, as recommended, the audit committee investigates thoroughly all financial aspects of the corporation's operations.

These very briefly constitute the major thrust of the Commission's recommendations in respect of boards. It is obvious that these go far beyond present practices, although they do not deal with some of the fundamental problems of power relationships dealt with in Chapter 7. However, if the Commission's recommendations were implemented it would alter radically present board practices in Canada and do a good deal to make it possible for boards to carry out the responsibilities outlined in Chapters 5 and 6.

III

The second model for reform is proposed by Melvin Eisenberg, Professor of Law at the University of California.[10] His analysis is at once more profound and far-reaching than that outlined above. Indeed, his analysis of corporate structure is both detailed and sophisticated, making any brief summary necessarily inadequate. Nonetheless, that which is most relevant for our purposes may, I think, be stated by underlining certain aspects of his major thesis.

Present corporate law is ambiguous and entirely unrealistic. He illustrates clearly why this is so and details many of the legal problems in this respect, of which the following are illustrative: the lack of differentiation between closely held corporations and widely held public corporations, the lack of clarity about the division of powers as between shareholders and directors, the ambiguity about the allocation

---

[10]Eisenberg, op. cit.

of powers among various corporate organs of a holding complex, the lack of validity of the statement that the board should "manage," the difficulty of interpreting what the law considers an "inside" versus an "outside" director, and the lack of clear definition of the role of the accountant in the corporate[11] structure. Many of these criticisms, I would suggest, apply to the Canada Business Corporations Act, and emphasize the importance and relevance of the *caveats* in Chapter 7.

Without going into his exhaustive proposals for change, it is possible to suggest that Eisenberg's major concepts are contained in the following:

1) He suggests that the division of power in the corporation should be related to the type of decision to be made. There are, he posits, four related types of decisions:

(a) Business decisions in the ordinary course. These would be decisions to hire and fire any but senior officers, the selection of suppliers, the price to be paid for materials, the assignment of duties to all but the CEO, and so on. These are decisions to be made by management, i.e., the senior officers of the company.

(b) Business decisions out of the ordinary course. These would be decisions such as expanding plant capacity, recognition of a particular trade union, developing a new but related product, and such matters as imply significant change in the corporation. These are in Eisenberg's view clearly board decisions.

(c) Decisions involving a substantial change in the structure of the enterprise. These involve such matters as the sale of major company assets, a merger with another enterprise, the purchase of another company, and such decisions as vitally affect the structure of the corporation. These are issues on which Eisenberg feels the directors should make the decisions but must consult the shareholders about the board's views.

(d) Decisions which affect the control apparatus of the corporation: that is, changes that would alter the by-laws, e.g., the number of directors, the proxy machinery, the kinds of information shareholders must receive, etc. Eisenberg views these decisions as the exclusive right of shareholders.

Such delineation of powers would unquestionably clarify the present uncertainties about responsibilities which have in law, and certainly in practice, been left ambiguous. One might disagree with this division of decision making but few would not recognize the very great need to clarify and standardize practice in this respect. Some

---

[11] Ibid.

lawsuits are against directors for taking actions which, some consider, exceed their authority. The law gives little guidance to a judge who must decide such an issue and of course officers, directors, and shareholders are often confused by the lack of clear definition of the responsibilities of each.

It should be said that Eisenberg makes a clear distinction between closely held corporations to which he gives considerable freedom and widely held corporations to which he applies many restrictions. "The underlying rule which should govern the internal affairs of closely held corporations is that the shareholders, acting unanimously, should be able to shape the corporate structure as they choose—business decisions in the ordinary course should be solely for the board; business decisions out of the ordinary course should be for the board but subject to intervention by the body of stockholders; and structural decisions should be solely for the shareholders acting by two-thirds majority."[12]

2) His next proposal is perhaps the most interesting and gives new status to the accounting profession—a status it may be reluctant to accept. After reviewing and analysing a variety of proposals for reform, such as full-time directors, directors with their own staff people, public directors, etc., he concludes that the vital and essential step necessary to give the board the information and authority it requires is the selection of independent auditors by the audit committee, who would be responsible not to management, but to the board. These auditors will apply their own accounting principles and will not be bound, as many of them now are, to acceptance of accounting principles developed by management. The accountants will have many responsibilities beyond present practice.

"Although the primary role of the accountant is to audit management's financial results, once the accountants have been made independent they will provide a capability enabling the board to audit managment's performance in other areas as well. Through this capability, for example, the board can acquire objective and reliable data not only on net profits, but on such benchmark indicators as market penetration and comparative costs. Going one step further, through this capability the board can audit the soundness of the corporation's underlying control systems, such as its capital- and operating-budget processes, cash and sales-forecasting techniques, and conflict-of-interest procedures. Finally, the capability brought to the board by truly independent accountants would enable it to evaluate management's

---

[12]Ibid., pp. 316-317.

results in meeting relevant nonfinancial objectives, such as compliance with law, due respect for the environment, provision of safe working conditions, nondiscrimination, and fair treatment of the consumer."[13]

These functions, Eisenberg claims, would not be completely new to accountants. Comparable audits have long been performed on behalf of government, and the profession has recently begun performing "management" or "operational audits" on behalf of business corporations. Until now, however, such audits have usually been performed as a service to management rather than as a check upon it.

There will be many who will question the validity of multi-functioning accountants, including some accounting firms. Perhaps the importance of this particular proposal is less in who (or what profession) is to investigate and report on these many matters than that the board should have independent knowledge about many aspects of the corporation for which it is responsible. Just as the accreditation committee of a hospital association provides the board of a particular hospital with information about all aspects of the hospital (information the board would unlikely acquire in the normal course), so the boards of profit corporations should be able to secure information from knowledgeable sources, free from the bias of management. If the law moves to increase directors' liability, such a move would seem sensible, if not inevitable.

IV

The third and final model of corporate structure carries the argument for increased board responsibility a good deal further. It is contained in Christopher Stone's book *Where the Law Ends: The Social Control of Corporate Behavior*.[14] Mr. Stone is professor of law at University of Southern California.

It is essential to understand the assumptions on the basis of which Stone's recommendations are made. For him, the corporation is not simply a business (or a service), a material thing, a profit-making operation, an educational or health service, but an organization that affects the attitudes, habits, behaviour patterns of individuals and groups as well as the values and the direction of our society. Many social scientists would support this view. Many Canadian corporations have budgets larger than that of some of the provinces and

---

[13] Ibid., pp. 210-211.

[14] Christopher Stone, *Where the Law Ends: The Social Control of Corporate Behavior* (New York: Harper & Row Publishers, 1975).

some of the multi-nationals have sales that exceed the federal budget in Canada.

Such corporations are of immense size and have tremendous influence in the lives of employees, suppliers, creditors, customers. It has been argued that governments are the major influence translating the social will into action, but Stone believes that the size and pervasiveness of the corporation has a profound impact on individual and social attitudes and goals—it is equal to the government in influence. It is critical for all of us, for example, whether honesty, responsibility, fairness, sensitivity to human and social values are the dominant practices of the corporation. The behaviour of the latter is a decisive force in our society.

Stone then argues, with numerous illustrations, that many corporations act irresponsibly and without due regard for the public good. He does not necessarily associate irresponsibility with dishonesty: "The person we deem irresponsible simply does not inform himself adequately about aspects of his environment that the responsible person observes. . . ."[16] For example, the National Institute of Mental Health has estimated that American pharmaceutical companies are manufacturing between 8 and 10 *billion* amphetamine pills each year. Many of these are shipped to Mexico, then smuggled back into the United States via an elaborate underground of illegal drug dealers. Stone's point is that pharmaceutical companies may not know this, may not choose to know it, or may only know about it in a very general way. Such companies should know about it in detail. Ignorance is not an excuse for irresponsibility. Applied generally to corporate boards this principle immensely expands the concept of directors' obligations. The responsible director must know what goes on in the corporation and how it affects society.

Stone argues further that the law is not adequate to deal with the many unsavoury incidents of corporate behaviour he identifies. This is because the major legal threat to a corporation is financial (the court cannot put a corporation in jail, order psychiatric treatment for it, etc.), and the fine is often relatively insignificant. Stone states that Ford made $350 million on the Mustang; it was fined $7 million for safety violations—relatively a very minor penalty. Furthermore, such fines are not seen in derogative fashion by corporate peers whose attitude seems to be "it could happen to anyone"—no stigma seems to be attached to these "mistakes."

---

[16]Stone, *op cit.*, p. 116.

Stone agrees with many others that the law is ambiguous and indeed "the law at times seems contradictory and therefore loses credibility." What is a prudent person? Who is an outside director? What subsidiaries are legal, ethical, and which merely "blind" to cover parent manipulations? Do directors "manage," "monitor," "guide," "advise," or "direct"? Even when the law is clear there is a tendency to ignore it, Stone argues, especially if one suspects a competitor of doing so, or one believes that one won't be caught. The conscientious corporate solicitor who advises caution is often considered troublesome, someone who "holds things up," and the CEO will seek out another lawyer who will "get things done."

From this rather negative view of the law and corporate behaviour, Stone proceeds to set down two fundamental requirements for the corporate director. This person is one who is: (a) committed to follow the law in a professional manner, that is, as a judge, doctor, or soldier, follow the law as they honestly understand it in terms of guiding their professional attitudes and activities, and (b) devoted to "the cognitive process" which goes far beyond mere obedience to the law or the rules, to involve such qualities as perception, restraint, awareness of accountability, sensitivity to consequences, weighing alternatives, reflection of "good and bad," "rights and duties," and far beyond to include what he terms "a moral vocabulary"—a moral disposition to do the right thing and to justify what one is doing in moral terms.

All this is prelude to Stone's detailed recommendations of the composition, duties, and proper functioning of the board of directors. Two types of board behaviour are required:

(a) Class A behaviour involves a board which if given adequate information can be counted upon to act honestly and with goals and values not inconsistent with the public interest. Such a board requires, in Stone's view, that companies of major impact (with sales of over $50 million) should be composed entirely of outsiders; a majority of directors should be financially disinterested (not financially associated with the company in business); should have a clear description of their role and duties; should have their own staff to provide information and analyse reports; and all classes of information should be available to it.

(b) Class B behaviour requires concern with a host of what Stone calls "public impacts": pollution, safety, health, labour, investment problems. To assure adequate attention to these matters new kinds of directors are required. In a situation where a corporation is found delinquent in some respect a special public director, who is an expert in that specific field of delinquency, should be appointed to study and report to the board on this problem. When it is resolved to the satisfaction of all, this special director may be removed from office.

Far more important is Stone's recommendation that Class B behaviour requires general public directors. These would be people nominated by the Federal Corporations Commission or the Security and Exchange Commission and approved, if found suitable, by the board of directors. The public directors would, presumably, represent the public interests, their number would be related to the size of the company (10% of the board for every one billion dollar of assets), would have an office in the corporation, would spend half time in the service of the board, and would be paid at the highest level of the civil service. Stone considers their value as being "an independent and probing and vigilant mind can contribute to board atmosphere—can raise impolite questions. . . ." Their functions are to assure the legitimacy of all aspects of corporate actions; to serve as an ombudsman for employees, stockholders, directors; to monitor the board's performance and to see that it fulfils its duties.

There are many executives and directors who can pinpoint many reasons why Stone's proposals are unrealistic and impractical. What must be noted, however, is that there is a body of opinion in Canada that would support these ideas. This group is distrustful of corporate behaviour and the lethargy of the small group of people who sit on corporate boards. And one must ask about those companies which were fined $6.6 million and their officers given jail sentences, in Canada's famous "rigging bids on dredging contracts"[17] case. Could this incident (not an isolated one by any means) have been prevented if the companies involved had a board composed mainly of outside directors, who had independent sources of information, and had as well one or more public directors sitting on the board of each company? This is not an easy question. Rather than dismiss Stone and his analysis, a better response would be to consider whether he does not have some justification for his proposals, and if his recommendations gall some, to ask how else one can achieve the ends he has set forth.

V

The value of these three models is they show in part, at least, the variety of recommendations being made for board reform. They, with additions, may be said to form the following spectrum:

---

[17]*The Globe and Mail*, 12 June 1979, pp. 1-2.

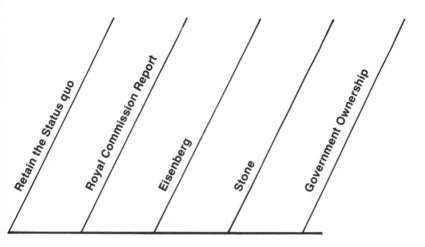

The spectrum starts at one extreme with those who are disinterested in change and want to retain the *status quo,* and extends to the other extreme, to those who would have the government take over all private enterprise and operate it "for the good of the people." The *status quo* position is no longer defensible; the desire for government ownership is anathema to many. The question is, then, where on this spectrum should reform begin?

It is worth emphasizing that which may not be obvious to all. The many calls for reform in the boardroom do not arise without cause. They are rooted in distrust and dissatisfaction with the structure of the corporation and the manner in which many boards operate. (Some reasons for this attitude were outlined in Chapter 1.) It is not possible to make judgments on the depth or extent of this dissatisfaction—whether it is growing or declining. But when one is confronted with a major Royal Commission Report and a detailed analysis by two leading intellectuals, all of which press for major reform in directorship practice, it would be folly to ignore the possibility of major external forces imposing their will on corporate boards. Almost all revolutions have been preceded by small numbers of intellectuals who have focused their interest and analytic ability on inadequacies or injustices in society and have written about these in a way that draws public attention.

Improving Board Performance in Canada

One study of the attitudes of 160 leaders in industry, finance, and government in the United States concluded that "they all reflect a certain anxiety and perplexity as to how public companies can live up to ever-higher expectations from the government, industry, and the public. They nearly all reflect an uneasy feeling that the old ground rules are shifting and no one knows how the new game will be played."[1] It is not surprising, therefore, that many managers and directors resist change and regard with nostalgia established practices which call for a routine board meeting for the hour prior to a pleasant directors' lunch.

The social turbulence of the sixties and the seventies has been sustained by the exposure of numerous unethical, if not illegal, corporate practices and the rise of entirely new public concerns about pollution, human rights, participatory democracy, full disclosure, etc. There is a lack of confidence in, if not distrust of, most traditional institutions, not the least of which is the corporation, its structure, its board of directors or trustees. Pressure for change in the boardroom is widespread, comes from many sources, and appears irresistible.

Unfortunately, the changes have to be made without knowing which specific changes are functional, feasible, productive. *We do not know,* for example, precisely where directors' activities interfere with management's responsibility and efficiency; nor do we know the specific areas where management may be usurping directors' functions. The role of directors as "managers of the affairs of the corporation" is fuzzy at best and is interpreted in different ways in various corporations. *We do not know* how much autonomy a subsidiary should have or can have. The duties of directors of the parent corporation may often be in conflict with the duties of directors of its subsidiaries. Funds may be diverted from Subsidiary A in order to save Subsidiary B. This may be to the disadvantage of Subsidiary A but to the advantage of the parent company and to Subsidiary B. What is the respon-

---

[1] Joseph W. Barr, "The Role of the Professional Director," *Harvard Business Review,* May-June 1976, p. 18.

sibility of directors of Company A? Should they—must they—accept this setback? The many questions that arise from parent-subsidiary relations remain largely unanswered either in law or in industry-wide practice. *We do not know* clearly what information is required beyond that which management provides its board—but which all experienced directors say is necessary—nor do we know precisely how such information can be obtained without causing internal friction. These and many other such questions merely underline the undeveloped state of knowledge about the governance of corporations. In many respects, in this critical area, we have been flying blind or as some would prefer to say, "by the seat of our pants."

There has been little research, apart from opinion polls, on corporate boards, so that the changes that are being made and that will be made will be less on the basis of careful investigation than on the basis of the judgment of those responsible and their response to pressures exerted by the public, security commissions, government, and the courts.

While, therefore, we have dogmatically outlined the duties of directors and made, and will make, proposals for change, it must be noted that these are suggestions based less on extensive research than on an attempt to balance the forces of a new era—the realities of our day, together with that which the law and experience has shown, are the necessities for effective board practice. The proposals are inevitably judgmental, value laden, and subjective.

1) *The Law:* At best, Canadian law is vague about many of the crucial areas of directors' responsibility. The most frequently quoted legal principle is that of Chief Justice Laskin in the *Canaero* case: "[T]he general standard of loyalty, good faith, and avoidance of conflict of duty and self-interest to which the conduct of a director or senior officer must conform, *must be tested in each case by many factors which it would be reckless to attempt to enumerate exhaustively.*"[2] To the layman, this is tantamount to saying that present law is not very clear, one cannot be certain precisely what one's responsibilities are as a director nor how the law will interpret them in any particular situation. Granted the difficulties of drafting legislation about the legal responsibilities of directors, it surely is not asking too much to require the law to be sufficiently clear to corporate lawyers, if not to laymen, who must in present circumstances accept vague legal obligations. Judgments by the courts previously reported provide some clues. They suggest a much more demanding standard of conduct on the part of

---

[2]Canaero v. O'Malley, *op. cit.*, p. 620.

directors. But if this is to be so, these standards need to be stated in law far more clearly than is now the case.

Further, the law is written to cover a wide variety of corporations, many of which have little in common. Particularly important would be to distinguish if there is a difference in the responsibility of the director of (a) a widely held corporation (b) a subsidiary corporation, and (c) a parent corporation. The law as written seems most applicable to corporations in the first group, i.e., the widely held corporation. But these regulations do not seem to apply equally to subsidiaries, however much law one can quote to support the opposite. The reality is that directors of subsidiaries are subject to anything from supervision and guidance to rigid control by those who own or control the subsidiary. Moreover, one may ask if the directors of huge conglomerates which control billions of dollars of assets, which can swallow and/or disgorge small corporations with ease, and which have tremendous influence on society, should not have more legal and higher moral responsibility than those in small or subsidiary corporations? Indeed one may ask, as Stone does, if there should not be a public presence on the board of such corporations. The law does not seem to differentiate between these quite different kinds of corporations.

It is one thing to require a formal structure for corporate governance (i.e., have shareholders, directors and managers) but quite another to provide assurance that the procedures that this structure implies are in fact functioning. James Baillie, Chairman of the Ontario Securities Commission, touched on this point in an important address on the new Securities Act.[3] Obviously he recognizes the importance of insisting that proper procedures be followed by management and directors. To date the law has little effect on those who ignore the intent of these procedures by simply passing the necessary "legal motions" prepared by the company solicitor. Amplification and clarification of the law in this respect would go a considerable distance in requiring directors to do their duty.

For these and other reasons one would hope that those scholars who specialize in corporate law will develop over the next few years proposals for reform that will be related to the realities of corporate life yet raise the standards of boardroom conduct.

2) *A Directors' Charter:* Most directors in profit and non-profit (except some in closely held profit) corporations would agree that the outline of directors' responsibilities (in Chapters 5 and 6) is "reasonable." But

---

[3]James C. Baillie, *op. cit.*

while these represent approximate agreement and while there is considerable written material that supports these proposals in whole or in part, there are very few corporations (profit or non-profit) that have endorsed a detailed and specific list of directors' responsibilities and incorporated them in their by-laws. What seems to be required is a *Charter of Directors' Rights and Responsibilities*. How else are directors, officers, shareholders, and the public to know what precisely is to be expected of directors? How else can directors be held accountable if there is a vagueness and an uncertainty about their duties?

Such an outline or charter might vary according to the type of corporation, but a clear statement on this subject in the by-laws would do much to give guidance to directors, to clarify for officers the territory and authority of the board, and to provide a path along which the board could move with certainty about its tasks and obligations. There is evidence that most directors have private interpretations of their responsibilities but that these private views differ in detail and sometimes in principle from director to director.[4] It is time for clarification and agreement. This does not mean more regulations—indeed it could mean fewer but more precise regulations. Many directors and officers, because of the vagueness but ever-present threat of the law, often now seem more concerned with passing motions to avoid lawsuits than with accomplishing the overall purpose of the organization.[5] What is required is a degree of simplicity in law and practice that is supported by a strong moral force which will make adhering to the charter of responsibilities a natural occurrence. It is rather surprising that corporate directors who seem unanimous in requiring job descriptions for others have never thought of providing one for themselves.

3) *External Aid:* James Madison wrote in 1822: "Knowledge will forever govern ignorance; and a people who mean to be their own governors, must arm themselves with the power knowledge gives."[6] If directors are "to govern" in any significant sense, they must have knowledge about the organization they are to govern. This is an essential first principal for directors.

As frequently mentioned previously, there is a growing body of opinion that boards require more information and advice about the corporation than they can reasonably expect from management. Sug-

---

[4]Peterson, op. cit.

[5]*Saturday Review*, 26 May 1979, p. 23.

[6]Quoted in *The Economist*, 5 May 1979, p. 132.

gestions to remedy this vary from freedom to consult the corporation's auditors and solicitor on an independent basis, to an auditor responsible to the board itself, to an independent staff for the board, to public directors, etc.

The minimum requirement here is an able, independent audit committee. It is difficult to imagine any substantial corporation, be it a university or a chain of supermarkets, whose directors do not need assurance that the figures they approve have been scrutinized in detail, and in consultation with outside auditors, by a small committee of their members. This is the very minimum for a modern board.

Going beyond this to employ a staff person(s) directly responsible to the board is to create inevitable conflict. All the evidence suggests petty jealousies and irritation arising between management and the board's staff person. A board which employs its own staff is creating a second source of information and advice which management may well resent. And what is the resolution of two different recommendations—one from the CEO and one from the board's staff? Is acceptance of the latter's view tantamount to a vote of non-confidence in the CEO? Most see the employment of a board staff member or a public director as a plan fraught with difficulties.[7]

And yet directors need to know much more about the complex corporations they control than most now do. In spite of the dangers involved, some of the proposals made by the Royal Commission, Eisenberg, Stone, and others must be considered. When CEOs of Canadian companies can make large donations to political parties or some questionable enterprise, without consulting the board of directors, and hide such donations under a budget heading such as "special payment," "in connection with legal and other affairs," or "miscellaneous payments,"[8] it is obvious that the board must, if it is to meet its responsibilities, find better means of ascertaining information about company affairs. An alert audit committee is one step in this direction, but obviously more is required. If one rejects the notion of a permanent board staff or of a public director (who would undoubtedly require a staff), some other means must be found for the board to obtain information and gain the knowledge it requires.

A less threatening method to management would be to decide to use an outside consultant(s) to study one or more divisions of the corporation in detail each year. Not many CEOs would object to such

---

[7]Barr, *op. cit.*, p. 18.

[8]See "Evidence Offers Rare Glimpse of Montreal's Big Business-Political Links," *The Globe and Mail*, 13 June 1979, pp. 1-2.

studies, particularly if they (management) took part in deciding the area(s) to be studied and the selection of the consultants. Over a period of years the board could become quite knowledgeable about the corporation as a result of regular studies and reports. It could well be that after discussion with management a study of the operation as a whole could be undertaken by outside experts, much as certifying and accrediting bodies study hospitals and university faculties.

There will not be a greater challenge to any board in the future than discovering the method best fitted to its own organization of providing any information it must have if it is to be effective.

4) *Expanded Duties:* There has been great demand in recent years from a variety of pressure groups for boards to expand their perspective and to concern themselves with a variety of social problems on which their corporations may have impact. There are numerous regulations now in place concerning the environment, marketing, disclosures, etc., that force consideration of these matters. But the pressure is still climbing.

It may seem unfair to expect a corporate board whose success is measured in terms of protecting shareholders' interests (which requires a fair return on investment), or a university whose board is charged with promoting learning and research, or a hospital whose board is primarily interested in patient care, to divert their attention from these purposes to give time and consideration to a whole host of problems which can only be seen as secondary issues.

But the reality is that boards must now be conscious of many concerns that could be ignored in the past. Trustees of pension and trust funds (in universities and labour unions) have gone so far as to withdraw investments in companies who do business with, or in, "unfavoured countries" or who take unpopular stands in labour negotiations.[9] In addition there are external pressures regarding pollution, health and safety, community projects for art, music, dance, etc. All of these add up to a very considerable group of demands to which boards are being asked to be attentive. Even such a conservative director as Courtney Brown admits that corporations will increasingly be required to provide "support and guidance from a board with interests in a growing array of concerns dealing with the external environment: community improvement, charitable giving, employee benefits, employee health and safety, minority and female hiring and promotion, environmental protection, shareholder democracy, and

---

[9]See Chapter 7, pp. 85-86.

even the determination of where to do business in a world of political and social tensions."[10] These are not, as often assumed, problems only for profit corporations, as universities, hospitals, and other such non-profit corporations are under the same pressures particularly with respect to hiring practices.

Whatever else was learned from the student uprisings in universities in the sixties, it was certain that it was folly to ignore or dismiss arbitrarily the demands or grievances of students no matter how irrational or silly these appeared to be. To do so was to aggravate the problem. It was far better to assume these were serious, if not legitimate, demands and to attempt to deal with them in reasonable fashion. A similar policy would not be amiss for the modern corporation. The criticisms and pressures of community groups may seem unreasonable to many directors, but an arbitrary dismissal of these is not likely to alleviate the criticisms or pressures. It is better to deal with these with reasoned argument. Perhaps the typical board reaction of rejection underlines the need for new directors who have a wider perspective, more knowledge, and a greater diversity of skills than those who now occupy the boardroom.

5) *Board Composition and Compensation:* There were many who felt that the University of Toronto had gone much too far when it had its Board of Governors abolished and turned over authority to manage the University to a Governing Council of over 50 members which included students, faculty, alumni, and government appointees. "It is like turning the lunatic asylum over to the inmates," one board member commented. But, after almost a decade, there is no evidence to suggest that the University of Toronto is a lesser institution than it once was, nor that it is operated less effectively than other universities with traditional boards. Similarly, the European experience with employee representation on the board of directors does not suggest lesser standards of profitability or less efficiency than would be the case without such representation.

The traditional criteria for board membership seems to relate to business status, knowledge, and influence; legal and banking experience; ability to get along with board colleagues; and capacity to enhance the reputation of the corporation. Such board members, with notable exceptions, have been able to judge "bottom-line" results and to provide advice that kept the corporation in a stable, if not a dynamic, position. Most CEOs and their management groups would

---

[10]Courtney C. Brown, *op. cit.,* p. 7.

argue that this is what they want—indeed all they want from a board.[11]

The pressure today is for a more open society—less secrecy, fewer private deals, less control by an elite. The public seems to be pressing corporations "to open up a little," to allow a few people who are not in the elite group to see what is going on, to permit a wider range of views to comment and vote on corporate policy and practice; in other words, to have boards whose composition represents many more views than the traditional business board.

There are strong arguments for and against such proposals. What must be remembered is that there is no evidence to suggest that broadening the composition of the board will in any way dilute the effectiveness of the board or lessen the efficiency of the corporation. Such experience as there is (at the University of Toronto, in Sweden and Germany, at General Motors in the United States)[12] indicates that corporations do not collapse because the base of board membership is broadened. Of course, it must be said also, that there is no evidence that such broadening improves board performance.[13] But it is important to emphasize that many of the fears about changing the composition of the board are, in fact, without foundation.

If, therefore, the reluctance of the CEOs can be overcome, it would seem an opportune time for corporations to relieve some of the suspicions about their "wheeling and dealing" by including as directors competent persons from sections of the community not usually associated with the corporate elite. Particularly important would be the boards of giant corporations which control many subsidiaries and whose directors tend to be closely related through business or friendship.

The Ontario and Federal Acts require two outside directors on the boards of corporations offering shares to the public. More useful would be a requirement that at least half the directors be outsiders,

---

[11] Barr, *op. cit.*, p. 18.

[12] A director and former President of one of General Motors companies told me that the appointment of a black minister (which resulted from pressure from the Ralph Nader group) had been a healthy and useful move, and that it had done "a great deal" to allay fears and suspicions about General Motors in the community.

[13] A new law passed in West Germany in 1976 requires all companies with more than 2,000 employees to have a corporate board with 50-50 representation of shareholders and workers (a regulation that previously applied only to the coal, iron, and steel industries). This has stirred much controversy and may aggravate labour-management relations there. See "Worker-director plan strains West Germany's industrial peace," *The Financial Post*, 8 September 1979, p. 14.

i.e., people independent of management. There have been tentative suggestions in Canada that a government agency, such as one of the security commissions, could be directed to select a panel from which outside directors could be appointed.[14] In any case, a strong argument can be made, in light of public attitudes, for including on the board outside directors who will provide balance in terms of age, sex, specialized knowledge, and skills.

It is interesting that a U.S. journal should record appreciatively that "in Canada, the first Eskimo was named to the board of directors of a corporation headquartered outside the Arctic area. This radical departure took place at Panartic Oils Ltd., an Arctic oil exploration company owned by the Canadian government and a consortium of 70 companies."[15] The author might be surprised to discover that in Canada such an appointment is extremely untypical.

For example, a study in 1972 showed that seven of the 126 companies reporting had women directors.[16] One would expect that because of the thrust of women in the business community in recent years, there would be a considerable change in this respect by 1979, but "despite women's recent inroads in business, they hold fewer than one percent of Canada's approximately 13,000 public and private company directorships, representing an extremely slight increase since . . . 1973 . . . by comparison 26 percent of corporate boards in the United States have female members, a 17 percent increase in the past five years."[17] This is more typical of the Canadian experience (than the appointment of an Eskimo director) which demonstrates either an unwillingness or an incapacity of the corporation to respond to the requirements of a more open society.

It should be said that non-profit corporations have been more progressive in this respect—especially in electing or appointing women members on their boards, although in many ways the major non-profit corporations are still dominated by the same people, or are employed by the same people, who sit on the boards of profit corporations.

Very few people sit on boards for the compensation provided. Indeed, this is desirable so that directors are not dependent on a fee,

---

[14]Jacobucci *et al, op cit,* p. 251.

[15]Stanley Vance, "New Dimensions for Boards of Directors," *Conference Board Record,* November 1971, p. 57.

[16]Morris Heath, *Size and Composition of Boards of Directors* (Ottawa: Conference Board in Canada), p. 1.

[17]Report on Business, *The Globe and Mail,* 23 July 1979, p. B1.

and at least for this reason can feel free to resign, if necessary, on a question of principle. Of course, directors of charitable non-profit organizations do not and should not be paid a fee. Their compensation is service to the community.

But in profit corporations where money is a factor, the amount of compensation is often related to the seriousness with which a job is undertaken. In 1972 a Conference Board study[18] showed only one manufacturing company paying a combined (retainer plus meeting fee) compensation for outside directors of over $10,000 and the median was in the $3,000 to $5,000 range. There is the impression that while outside director fees remained static for many years, gradual increases were provided since 1972.[19] But a 1976 study showed that "the median annual compensation for outside directors in all manufacturing and non-manufacturing companies was only $3,750."

In addition board members in most companies receive fees for committee service, the median being about $250 per meeting, but higher fees in some companies for service on the executive or audit committees. In spite of this it seems few directors receive more than $6,000 per year in total for their service as directors of any but the largest companies.[20] Admittedly, if outside directors are to perform as suggested here, and if they are to confine their attention to only one or two boards, a dramatic increase in compensation would seem to be indicated. If the position of directors of a profit company is important, the compensation should reflect this fact. A fee in the $10,000 to $20,000 range does not seem unreasonable.

The change has already begun in the United States where "corporations in the $1 billion plus sales range are now paying their outside directors between $15,000 and $25,000 per year, while those with $100 million to $1 billion in sales generally pay between $7,500 and $15,000."[21]

6) *The Chairman:* Some very able observers of board operations believe that the separation of the role of chairman from that of the CEO

---

[18]Robert van Eyck, *Compensation of Boards of Directors* (Ottawa: The Conference Board in Canada, 1974), p. 7.

[19]Ibid., p. 24.

[20]Ian Watson and Kenneth Wong, *Canadian Directorship Practices: Compensation 1976* (Ottawa, Conference Board in Canada, 1976).

[21]Robert W. Lear, "Compensation for Outside Directors," *Harvard Business Review,* November-December 1979, p. 18.

is vital to the successful board.[22] The lesson of non-profit corporations, particularly hospitals and universities, is instructive here. Some outside chairmen have given great amounts of time and made very significant contributions to such organizations. Why not to profit corporations? It is quite possible that the chairman could relieve the CEO of a good deal of board work, could assure the board that the essential items were on the agenda, that adequate information was available, and could by his very presence and status assure objective consideration of the problems at hand. One can think of such persons as J. G. Hungerford of National Trust, who served as Chairman of the Board of Canada Life, John Taylor of Liquifuels, Chairman of North American Life Assurance Company, and Malim Harding of Harding Carpets, who serves as Chairman of Union Gas, as people who made and make such a contribution. It appears critical to many of the reforms suggested here to separate the functions of the corporation's management and operating people from those of the board. The former should report to the board—not control it. This would also terminate the practice of promoting the retiring CEO to chairman of the board. A fresh outside person of status and skill can, as chairman, undoubtedly bring new vigour and insights to the board. If "checks and balances" are necessary in government and in society, they are also essential in the boardroom. Separate powers for the chairman and the CEO go some way to provide for this.

7) *The CEO:* My own experience leads me to believe that the CEO is a most important determinant of how well a board functions. If, as indicated earlier, this person regards the board as a nuisance, or as a threat, or as a mere formality, he can have a profound negative influence on the board. This is because he is at present the major funnel through which the board obtains information. This officer has a hundred ways in which he can hide the facts, slant information, deny relevant data, etc. If his attitude is hostile or passive it is extremely difficult for the board to function as it should.

There is evidence to suggest that when outside directors are involved, this negative attitude on the part of the CEO tends to persist. One study of such attitudes reported: "There was an undercurrent in many of their replies that could be paraphrased, 'We wish to God, that we did not have any outside directors, but especially no professional directors.' "[23] Such CEOs do not seem to realize that this atti-

---

[22]Courtney C. Brown, *op. cit.,* pp. 42-43, 102.

[23]Barr, *op cit.,* p. 19.

tude can only result in a responsible board (or society) insisting on other sources of information—a greater dependence on outside auditors, lawyers, perhaps even the election of professional directors.

On the other hand, if the CEO recognizes and accepts the authority of the board, acknowledges its need for full and complete information on all major issues, and if he co-operates fully with the chairman and the board in "a partnership relationship" of mutual concern for the welfare of the corporation, he can thereby greatly enhance the work of the board, and his own prestige.

The attitude of the CEO is therefore critical. But even if his attitude is positive, he requires skill in working with his board. He should stimulate interest, encourage participation, seek advice, ask questions, explain his problems, admit his mistakes, etc., not in a servile manner but as a partner in a common enterprise.

In some profit corporations the CEO is given such status that he dominates the board. With salaries and benefits from $300,000 to $450,000 annually,[24] these CEOs probably have greater financial clout than many of their directors, and salaries are meant to reflect their responsibilities—to run the company! This conception of the role of the CEO inevitably erodes board authority. It can only be aborted by board members who insist on carrying out their responsibilities by not accepting the dominance of any one person on the board.

Donald Perkins, the CEO of the Jewel Companies and a director of a number of major U.S. companies, outlined what his directors have a right to expect of him as CEO.[25] His statement provides useful advice for all serious CEOs. The board has a right to expect:

1) The achievement of results consistent with our internal plans and our external environment.
2) The attraction and development of successor managers, periodic commentary about them, and occasional opportunity to observe these high potential individuals in action.
3) Maintaining and emphasizing Jewel's reputation of honesty and integrity.
4) Keeping our physical facilities and our operating systems up-to-date.
5) Reassurance that the company's financial statements are accurate and that its assets are safeguarded.
6) Balancing the conflicting demands of short- and long-term

---

[24]"The Top Dozen Salaries," *The Financial Post*, 9 June 1979, p. 1.

[25]Donald S. Perkins, "What the CEO and Board Expect of Each Other," *Harvard Business Review*, March-April 1979, p. 26.

pressures and balancing the conflicting demands of our share-holders, customers, and employees.

7) . . . me to remember that I am a company employee.
8) . . . me to operate in a style consistent with our concern for people.
9) . . . regular communication about problems as well as achievements.
10) . . . me to show respect for their time.
11) . . . a certain quality and style of board meetings. Ample time for discussion of whatever they want to talk about is a must.
12) . . . me to welcome their involvement and oversight.

If these obligations are observed, it will do much to encourage effective board work.

II

That which most inhibits change in the boardroom are those officers and directors who are content with present practices. This attitude flies in the face of the underlying philosophy of corporate structure which was designed to decentralize power and to provide for a system of balances and restraints. It also flies in the face of a growing public opinion that insists the corporation be more open in its operations and that a greater variety of voices be heard in the forming of corporate policy.

These requirements and pressures may be ignored temporarily. But with all the evidence from changing board practices in the United States, from the increasing activity of security commissions in Canada, from governments sensitive to the demands of many pressure groups, from scholars of corporate law, and from recent judgments in Canadian courts, the cumulative effect will be to require change. To resist "the handwriting on the wall" reminds one of the Russian priests in conference to discuss proper clerical dress while the great revolution of 1917 was beginning. Changes there will be; directors and their corporations should recognize and adapt to them.

To judge from the variety of studies, discussions, and comments, the following changes, as a minimum, appear to be necessary:

—A rewriting and clarification of the law. At present there are far too many ambiguities in the law—from the meaning of "to manage" to the responsibilities of directors of subsidiaries. Recent decisions suggest a new and firmer attitude on the part of our courts, but it is not a judge's duty to make the law. For the sake of the courts, the public, and corporate directors the law should be rewritten to reflect new demands being made on corporations and to clarify the duties of directors.

—A higher percentage of independent outside directors— "independent" in the sense that they are free of financial, family, and friendship obligations to the corporation and its management; "outside" in the sense that they are not officers or former officers of the company nor are they paid advisors of the corporations.

—A more secure source of information than that which is provided by management. Accountants, solicitors, consultants who are independent of management and directly responsible to the board are more acceptable at the moment than an independent board staff or professional directors.

—A chairman of the board who is not an officer or former officer of the corporation. A clear division of responsibilities for the chairman and the CEO is desirable.

A more profound change is required if one accepts Stone's analysis of the influence of the corporation on social attitudes and values. He views corporations as social institutions with great impact on individuals and on society and therefore required to be subject to a degree of social input and control. Giant multi-national corporations and huge conglomerates are relatively new developments in our society to which attention only recently has been given. The Royal Commission on Corporate Concentration concluded that, at present, there was not undue concentration of corporations in Canada. Even if one accepts this judgment (and many do not) one must recognize the tremendous authority of the boards of these billion dollar enterprises.

In the Canadian context, accepting Stone's thesis would require as a minimum:

—that all large subsidiaries with sales or assets of over (say) $50 million have a board with a majority of Canadian outside directors who have all the rights and responsibilities of an independent board.

—that the boards of parent companies in Canada (CP, Hollinger-Argus, Power, etc.) have on their board "a public presence," that is, a number of directors selected from a panel prepared by a security commission or government agency, which would provide some assurance that corporate policy was subject to scrutiny by a few persons other than the traditional and closely knit group of business directors.

EXCERPT FROM CANADA BUSINESS CORPORATIONS ACT*

PART IX

DIRECTORS AND OFFICERS

Power to manage

97. (1) Subject to any unanimous shareholder agreement, the directors shall manage the business and affairs of a corporation.

Number of directors

(2) A corporation shall have one or more directors but a corporation, any of the issued securities of which are or were part of a distribution to the public, shall have not fewer than three directors, at least two of whom are not officers or employees of the corporation or its affiliates.

By-laws

98. (1) Unless the articles, by-laws or a unanimous shareholder agreement otherwise provide, the directors may, by resolution make, amend, or repeal any by-laws that regulate the business or affairs of the corporation.

Shareholder approval

(2) The directors shall submit a by-law, or an amendment or a repeal of a by-law, made under subsection (1) to the shareholders at the next meeting of shareholders, and the shareholders may, by ordinary resolution, confirm, reject or amend the by-law, amendment or repeal.

Effective date

(3) A by-law, or an amendment or a repeal of a by-law, is effective from the date of the resolution of the directors under subsection (1) until it is confirmed, confirmed as amended or rejected by the shareholders under subsection (2) or until it ceases to be effective under subsection (4) and, where the by-law is confirmed or confirmed as amended, it continues in effect in the form in which it was so confirmed.

*Canada Business Corporations Act, Chap. 33 (1974-75), Vol. 1, No. 6, *Canada Gazette* Part III, pp. 68-88. Reproduced by permission of Minister of Supply and Services Canada.

Idem

(4) If a by-law, an amendment or a repeal is rejected by the shareholders, or if the directors do not submit a by-law, an amendment or a repeal to the shareholders as required under subsection (2), the by-law, amendment or repeal ceases to be effective and no subsequent resolution of the directors to make, amend or repeal a by-law having substantially the same purpose or effect is effective until it is confirmed or confirmed as amended by the shareholders.

Shareholder proposal

(5) A shareholder may, in accordance with section 131, make a proposal to make, amend or repeal a by-law.

Organization meeting

99. (1) After issue of the certificate of incorporation, a meeting of the directors of the corporation shall be held at which the directors may

(*a*) make by-laws;

(*b*) adopt forms of security certificates and corporate records;

(*c*) authorize the issue of securities;

(*d*) appoint officers;

(*e*) appoint an auditor to hold office until the first annual meeting of shareholders;

(*f*) make banking arrangements; and

(*g*) transact any other business.

Calling meeting

(2) An incorporator or a director may call the meeting of directors referred to in subsection (1) by giving not less than five days notice thereof by mail to each director, stating the time and place of the meeting.

Qualifications of directors

100. (1) The following persons are disqualified from being a director of a corporation:

(*a*) anyone who is less than eighteen years of age;

(*b*) anyone who is of unsound mind and has been so found by a court in Canada or elsewhere;

(*c*) a person who is not an individual; or

(*d*) a person who has the status of bankrupt.

Further qualifications

(2) Unless the articles otherwise provide, a director of a corporation is not required to hold shares issued by the corporation.

Residency

(3) A majority of the directors of a corporation must be resident Canadians.

Exception for holding corporation

(4) Notwithstanding subsection (3), not more than one-third of the directors of a holding corporation need be resident Canadians if the holding corporation earns in Canada directly or through its subsidiaries less than five per cent of the gross revenues of the holding corporation and all of its subsidiary bodies corporate together as shown in the most recent consolidated financial statements of the holding corporation or the most recent financial statements of the holding corporation and its subsidiary bodies corporate.

Notice of directors

101. (1) At the time of sending articles of incorporation, the incorporators shall send to the Director a notice of directors in prescribed form and the Director shall file the notice.

Term of office

(2) Each director named in the notice referred to in subsection (1) holds office from the issue of the certificate of incorporation until the first meeting of shareholders.

Election of directors

(3) Subject to paragraph 102(b), shareholders of a corporation shall, by ordinary resolution at the first meeting of shareholders and at each succeeding annual meeting at which an election of directors is required, elect directors to hold office for a term expiring not later than the close of the third annual meeting of shareholders following the election.

Staggered terms

(4) It is not necessary that all directors elected at a meeting of shareholders hold office for the same term.

No stated terms

(5) A director not elected for an expressly stated term ceases to hold office at the close of the first annual meeting of shareholders following his election.

Incumbent directors

(6) Notwithstanding subsections (2), (3) and (5), if directors are not elected at a meeting of shareholders the incumbent directors continue in office until their successors are elected.

Vacancy among candidates

(7) If a meeting of shareholders fails to elect the number or the minimum number of directors

required by the articles by reason of the disqualification, incapacity or death of any candidates, the directors elected at that meeting may exercise all the powers of the directors if the number of directors so elected constitutes a quorum.

Cumulative
voting

102. Where the articles provide for cumulative voting,

(*a*) the articles shall require a fixed number and not a minimum and maximum number of directors;

(*b*) each shareholder entitled to vote at an election of directors has the right to cast a number of votes equal to the number of votes attached to the shares held by him multiplied by the number of directors to be elected, and he may cast all such votes in favour of one candidate or distribute them among the candidates in any manner;

(*c*) a separate vote of shareholders shall be taken with respect to each candidate nominated for director unless a resolution is passed unanimously permitting two or more persons to be elected by a single resolution;

(*d*) If a shareholder has voted for more than one candidate without specifying the distribution of his votes among the candidates, he is deemed to have distributed his votes equally among the candidates for whom he voted;

(*e*) if the number of candidates nominated for director exceeds the number of positions to be filled, the candidates who receive the least number of votes shall be eliminated until the number of candidates remaining equals the number of positions to be filled;

(*f*) each director ceases to hold office at the close of the first annual meeting of shareholders following his election;

(*g*) a director may not be removed from office if the votes cast against his removal would be sufficient to elect him and such votes could be voted cumulatively at an election at which the same total number of votes were cast and the number of directors required by the articles were then being elected; and (*h*) the number of directors required by the articles may not be decreased if the votes cast against the motion to decrease would be sufficient to elect a director and such votes could be voted cumulatively at an election at which the same total number of votes were cast and the number of directors required by the articles were then being elected.

Ceasing to hold office

103. (1) A director of a corporation ceases to hold office when

(*a*) he dies or resigns;

(*b*) he is removed in accordance with section 104; or

(*c*) he becomes disqualified under subsection 100(1).

Effective date of resignation

(2) A resignation of a director becomes effective at the time a written resignation is sent to the corporation, or at the time specified in the resignation, whichever is later.

Removal of directors

104. (1) Subject to paragraph 102(*g*), the shareholders of a corporation may by ordinary resolution at a special meeting remove any director or directors from office.

Exception

(2) Where the holders of any class or series of shares of a corporation have an exclusive right to elect one or more directors, a director so elected may only be removed by an ordinary resolution at a meeting of the shareholders of that class or series.

Vacancy

(3) Subject to paragraphs 102(*b*) to (*e*), a vacancy created by the removal of a director may be filled at the meeting of the shareholders at which the director is removed or, if not so filled, may be filled under section 106.

Attendance at meeting

105. (1) A director of a corporation is entitled to receive notice of and to attend and be heard at every meeting of shareholders.

Statement of director

(2) A director who

(*a*) resigns,

(*b*) receives a notice or otherwise learns of a meeting of shareholders called for the purpose of removing him from office, or (*c*) receives a notice or otherwise learns of a meeting of directors or shareholders at which another person is to be appointed or elected to fill the office of director, whether because of his resignation or removal or because his term of office has expired or is about to expire,

is entitled to submit to the corporation a written statement giving the reasons for his resignation or the reasons why he opposes any proposed action or resolution.

Circulating statement

(3) A corporation shall forthwith send a copy of the statement referred to in subsection (2) to every shareholder entitled to receive notice of any meeting referred to in subsection (1) and to the Director unless the statement is included in or attached to a management proxy circular required by section 144.

Immunity

(4) No corporation or person acting on its behalf incurs any liability by reason only of circulating a director's statement in compliance with subsection (3).

Filling vacancy

106. (1) Notwithstanding subsection 109(3), but subject to subsections (3) and (4), a quorum of directors may fill a vacancy among the directors, except a vacancy resulting from an increase in the number or minimum number of directors or from a failure to elect the number or minimum number of directors required by the articles.

Calling meeting

(2) If there is not a quorum of directors, or if there has been a failure to elect the number or minimum number of directors required by the articles, the directors then in office shall forthwith call a special meeting of shareholders to fill the vacancy and, if they fail to call a meeting or if there are no directors then in office, the meeting may be called by any shareholder.

Class director

(3) Where the holders of any class or series, of shares of a corporation have an exclusive right to elect one or more directors and a vacancy occurs among those directors,

(*a*) subject to subsection (4), the remaining directors elected by that class or series may fill the vacancy except a vacancy resulting from an increase in the number or minimum number of directors for that class or series or from a failure to elect the number or minimum number of directors for that class or series; or

(b) if there are no such remaining directors any holder of shares of that class or series may call a meeting of the holders thereof for the purpose of filling the vacancy.

Shareholders filing vacancy

(4) The articles may provide that a vacancy among the directors shall only be filled by a vote of the shareholders, or by a vote of the holders of any class or series of shares having an exclusive right to elect one or more directors if the vacancy occurs among the directors elected by that class or series.

Unexpired term

(5) A director appointed or elected to fill a vacancy holds office for the unexpired term of his predecessor.

Number of directors

107. The shareholders of a corporation may amend the articles to increase or, subject to paragraph 102(h), to decrease the number of directors, or the minimum or maximum number of directors, but no decrease shall shorten the term of an incumbent director.

Notice of change of directors

108. (1) Within fifteen days after a change is made among its directors, a corporation shall send to the Director a notice in prescribed form setting out the change and the Director shall file the notice.

Application to court

(2) Any interested person, or the Director, may apply to a court for an order to require a corporation to comply with subsection (1), and the court may so order and make any further order it thinks fit.

Meeting of directors

109. (1) Unless the articles or by-laws otherwise provide, the directors may meet at any place, and upon such notice as the by-laws require.

Quorum

(2) Subject to the articles or by-laws, a majority of the number of directors or minimum number of directors required by the articles constitutes a quorum at any meeting of directors,

and, notwithstanding any vacancy among the directors, a quorum of directors may exercise all the powers of the directors.

Canadian majority

(3) Directors, other than directors of a corporation referred to in subsection 100(4), shall not transact business at a meeting of directors unless a majority of directors present are resident Canadians.

Exception

(4) Notwithstanding subsection (3), directors may transact business at a meeting of directors where a majority of resident Canadian directors is not present if

(a) a resident Canadian director who is unable to be present approves in writing or by telephone or other communications facilities the business transacted at the meeting; and

(b) a majority of resident Canadian directors would have been present had that director been present at the meeting.

Notice of meeting

(5) A notice of a meeting of directors shall specify any matter referred to in subsection 110(3) that is to be dealt with at the meeting but, unless the by-laws otherwise provide, need not specify the purpose of or the business to be transacted at the meeting.

Waiver of notice

(6) A director may in any manner waive a notice of a meeting of directors; and attendance of a director at a meeting of directors is a waiver of notice of the meeting, except where a director attends a meeting for the express purpose of objecting to the transaction of any business on the grounds that the meeting is not lawfully called.

Adjournment

(7) Notice of an adjourned meeting of directors is not required to be given if the time and place of the adjourned meeting is announced at the original meeting.

One director meeting

(8) Where a corporation has only one director, that director may constitute a meeting.

Participation by telephone

(9) Subject to the by-laws, a director may, if all the directors of the corporation consent, participate in a meeting of directors or of a committee of directors by means of such telephone or other communications facilities as permit all

persons participating in the meeting to hear each other, and a director participating in such a meeting by such means is deemed for the purposes of this Act to be present at that meeting.

Delegation

110. (1) Directors of a corporation may appoint from their number a managing director who is a resident Canadian or a committee of directors and delegate to such managing director or committee any of the powers of the directors.

Canadian majority

(2) If the directors of a corporation, other than a corporation referred to in subsection 100(4), appoint a committee of directors, a majority of the members of the committee must be resident Canadians.

Limits on authority

(3) Notwithstanding subsection (1), no managing director and no committee of directors has authority to

(*a*) submit to the shareholders any question or matter requiring the approval of the shareholders;

(*b*) fill a vacancy among the directors or in the office of auditor;

(*c*) issue securities except in the manner and on the terms authorized by the directors;

(*d*) declare dividends;

(*e*) purchase, redeem or otherwise acquire shares issued by the corporation;

(*f*) pay a commission referred to in section 39;

(*g*) approve a management proxy circular referred to in Part XII;

(*h*) approve a take-over bid circular or directors' circular referred to in Part XVI;

(*i*) approve any financial statements referred to in section 149; or

(*j*) adopt, amend or repeal by-laws.

Validity of acts of directors and officers

111. An act of a director or officer is valid notwithstanding an irregularity in his election or appointment or a defect in his qualification.

Resolution in lieu of meeting

112. (1) A resolution in writing, signed by all the directors entitled to vote on that resolution at a meeting of directors or committee of directors, is as valid as if it had been passed at a meeting of directors or committee of directors.

Filing
resolution

(2) A copy of every resolution referred to in subsection (1) shall be kept with the minutes of the proceedings of the directors or committee of directors.

Directors'
liability

113. (1) Directors of a corporation who vote for or consent to a resolution authorizing the issue of a share under section 25 for a consideration other than money are jointly and severally liable to the corporation to make good any amount by which the consideration received is less than the fair equivalent of the money that the corporation would have received if the share had been issued for money on the date of the resolution.

Further
directors'
liabilities

(2) Directors of a corporation who vote for or consent to a resolution authorizing

(*a*) a purchase, redemption or other acquisition of shares contrary to section 32, 33 or 34,

(*b*) a commission contrary to section 39,

(*c*) a payment of a dividend contrary to section 40,

(*d*) financial assistance contrary to section 42,

(*e*) a payment of an indemnity contrary to section 119, or

(*f*) a payment to a shareholder contrary to section 184 or 234,

are jointly and severally liable to restore to the corporation any amounts so distributed or paid and not otherwise recovered by the corporation.

Contribution

(3) A director who has satisfied a judgment rendered under this section is entitled to contribution from the other directors who voted for or consented to the unlawful act upon which the judgment was founded.

Recovery

(4) A director liable under subsection (2) is entitled to apply to a court for an order compelling a shareholder or other recipient to pay or

deliver to the director any money or property that was paid or distributed to the shareholder or other recipient contrary to section 32, 33, 34, 39, 40, 42, 119, 184 or 234.

Order
of court

(5) In connection with an application under subsection (4) a court may, if it is satisfied that it is equitable to do so,

(a) order a shareholder or other recipient to pay or deliver to a director any money or property that was paid or distributed to the shareholder or other recipient contrary to section 32, 33, 34, 39, 40, 42, 119, 184 or 234;

(b) order a corporation to return or issue shares to a person from whom the corporation has purchased, redeemed or otherwise acquired shares; or

(c) make any further order it thinks fit.

No
liability

(6) A director is not liable under subsection (1) if he proves that he did not know and could not reasonably have known that the share was issued for a consideration less than the fair equivalent of the money that the corporation would have received if the share had been issued for money.

Limitation

(7) An action to enforce a liability imposed by this section may not be commenced after two years from the date of the resolution authorizing the action complained of.

Liability of
directors for
wages

114. (1) Directors of a corporation are jointly and severally liable to employees of the corporation for all debts not exceeding six months wages payable to each such employee for services performed for the corporation while they are such directors respectively.

Conditions
precedent to
liability

(2) A director is not liable under subsection (1) unless

(a) the corporation has been sued for the debt within six months after it has become due and execution has been returned unsatisfied in whole or in part;

(b) the corporation has commenced liquidation and dissolution proceedings or has been dissolved and a claim for the debt has been proved within six months after the earlier of the date of commencement of the liquidation and dissolution proceedings and the date of dissolution; or

(c) the corporation has made an assignment or a receiving order has been made against it under the *Bankruptcy Act* and a claim for the debt has been proved within six months after the date of the assignment or receiving order.

Limitation

(3) A director is not liable under this section unless he is sued for a debt referred to in subsection (1) while he is a director or within two years after he has ceased to be a director.

Amount due after execution

(4) Where execution referred to in paragraph (2) (a) has issued, the amount recoverable from a director is the amount remaining unsatisfied after execution.

Subrogation of director

(5) Where a director pays a debt referred to in subsection (1) that is proved in liquidation and dissolution or bankruptcy proceedings, he is entitled to any preference that the employee would have been entitled to, and where a judgment has been obtained he is entitled to an assignment of the judgment.

Contribution

(6) A director who has satisfied a claim under this section is entitled to contribution from the other directors who were liable for the claim.

Disclosure of interested director contract

115. (1) A director or officer of a corporation who

(a) is a party to a material contract or proposed material contract with the corporation, or

(b) is a director or an officer of or has a material interest in any person who is a party to a material contract or proposed material contract with the corporation,

shall disclose in writing to the corporation or request to have entered in the minutes of meetings of directors the nature and extent of his interest.

Time of disclosure for director

(2) The disclosure required by subsection (1) shall be made, in the case of a director,

(*a*) at the meeting at which a proposed contract is first considered;

(*b*) if the director was not then interested in a proposed contract, at the first meeting after he becomes so interested;

(*c*) if the director becomes interested after a contract is made, at the first meeting after he becomes so interested; or

(*d*) if a person who is interested in a contract later becomes a director, at the first meeting after he becomes a director.

Time of disclosure for officer

(3) The disclosure required by subsection (1) shall be made, in the case of an officer who is not a director,

(*a*) forthwith after he becomes aware that the contract or proposed contract is to be considered or has been considered at a meeting of directors;

(*b*) if the officer becomes interested after a contract is made, forthwith after he becomes so interested; or

(*c*) if a person who is interested in a contract later becomes an officer, forthwith after he becomes an officer.

Time of disclosure for director or officer

(4) If a material contract or proposed material contract is one that, in the ordinary course of the corporation's business, would not require approval by the directors or shareholders, a director or officer shall disclose in writing to the corporation or request to have entered in the minutes of meetings of directors the nature and extent of his interest forthwith after the director or officer becomes aware of the contract or proposed contract.

Voting

(5) A director referred to in subsection (1) shall not vote on any resolution to approve the contract unless the contract is

(*a*) an arrangement by way of security for money lent to or obligations undertaken by him for the benefit of the corporation or an affiliate;

(*b*) one relating primarily to his remuneration as a director, officer, employee or agent of the corporation or an affiliate;

(*c*) one for indemnity or insurance under section 119; or

(*d*) one with an affiliate.

Continuing
disclosure

(6) For the purposes of this section, a general notice to the directors by a director or officer, declaring that he is a director or officer of or has a material interest in a person and is to be regarded as interested in any contract made with that person, is a sufficient declaration of interest in relation to any contract so made.

Avoidance
standards

(7) A material contract between a corporation and one or more of its directors or officers, or between a corporation and another person of which a director or officer of the corporation is a director or officer or in which he has a material interest, is neither void nor voidable by reason only of that relationship or by reason only that a director with an interest in the contract is present at or is counted to determine the presence of a quorum at a meeting of directors or committee of directors that authorized the contract, if the director or officer disclosed his interest in accordance with subsection (2), (3), (4) or (6), as the case may be, and the contract was approved by the directors or the shareholders and it was reasonable and fair to the corporation at the time it was approved.

Application
to court

(8) Where a director or officer of a corporation fails to disclose his interest in a material contract in accordance with this section, a court may, upon the application of the corporation or a shareholder of the corporation, set aside the contract on such terms as it thinks fit.

Officers

116. Subject to the articles, the by-laws or any unanimous shareholder agreement,

(*a*) the directors may designate the offices of the corporation, appoint as officers persons of full capacity, specify their duties and delegate to them powers to manage the business and affairs of the corporation, except powers to do anything referred to in subsection 110(3);

(*b*) a director may be appointed to any office of the corporation; and

(*c*) two or more offices of the corporation may be held by the same person.

Duty of care of directors and officers

117. (1) Every director and officer of a corporation in exercising his powers and discharging his duties shall

(*a*) act honestly and in good faith with a view to the best interests of the corporation; and

(*b*) exercise the care, diligence and skill that a reasonably prudent person would exercise in comparable circumstances.

Duty to comply

(2) Every director and officer of a corporation shall comply with this Act, the regulations, articles, by-laws and any unanimous shareholder agreement.

No exculpation

(3) No provision in a contract, the articles, the by-laws or a resolution relieves a director or officer from the duty to act in accordance with this Act or the regulations or relieves him from liability for a breach thereof.

Dissent

118. (1) A director who is present at a meeting of directors or committee of directors is deemed to have consented to any resolution passed or action taken thereat unless

(*a*) he requests that his dissent be or his dissent is entered in the minutes of the meeting;

(*b*) he sends his written dissent to the secretary of the meeting before the meeting is adjourned; or

(*c*) he sends his dissent by registered mail or delivers it to the registered office of the corporation immediately after the meeting is adjourned.

Loss of right to dissent

(2) A director who votes for or consents to a resolution is not entitled to dissent under subsection (1).

Dissent of absent director

(3) A director who was not present at a meeting at which a resolution was passed or action taken is deemed to have consented thereto unless within seven days after he becomes aware of the resolution he

(*a*) causes his dissent to be placed with the minutes of the meeting; or

(*b*) sends his dissent by registered mail or delivers it to the registered office of the corporation.

Reliance on
statements

(4) A director is not liable under section 113, 114 or 117 if he relies in good faith upon

(*a*) financial statements of the corporation represented to him by an officer of the corporation or in a written report of the auditor of the corporation fairly to reflect the financial condition of the corporation; or

(*b*) a report of a lawyer, accountant, engineer, appraiser or other person whose profession lends credibility to a statement made by him.

Indemnification

119. (1) Except in respect of an action by or on behalf of the corporation or body corporate to procure a judgment in its favour, a corporation may indemnify a director or officer of the corporation, a former director or officer of the corporation or a person who acts or acted at the corporation's request as a director or officer of a body corporate of which the corporation is or was a shareholder or creditor, and his heirs and legal representatives, against all costs, charges and expenses, including an amount paid to settle an action or satisfy a judgment, reasonably incurred by him in respect of any civil, criminal or administrative action or proceeding to which he is made a party by reason of being or having been a director of officer of such corporation or body corporate, if

(*a*) he acted honestly and in good faith with a view to the best interests of the corporation; and

(*b*) in the case of a criminal or administrative action or proceeding that is enforced by a monetary penalty, he had reasonable grounds for believing that his conduct was lawful.

Indemnification in derivative actions

(2) A corporation may with the approval of a court indemnify a person referred to in subsection (1) in respect of an action by or on behalf of the corporation or body corporate to procure a judgment in its favour, to which he is made a party by reason of being or having been a director or an officer of the corporation or body corporate, against all costs, charges and expenses reasonably incurred by him in connection with

such action if he fulfils the conditions set out in paragraphs (1) (*a*) and (*b*).

(3) Notwithstanding anything in this section, a corporation shall indemnify any person referred to in subsection (1) who has been substantially successful in the defence of any civil, criminal or administrative action or proceeding to which he is made a party by reason of being or having been a director or officer of the corporation or body corporate against all costs, charges and expenses reasonably incurred by him in respect of such action or proceedings.

(4) A corporation may purchase and maintain insurance for the benefit of any person referred to in this section against any liability incurred by him under paragraph 117(1) (*b*) in his capacity as a director or officer of the corporation.

(5) A corporation or a person referred to in subsection (1) may apply to a court for an order approving an indemnity under this section and the court may so order and make any further order it thinks fit.

(6) An applicant under subsection (5) shall give the Director notice of the application and the Director is entitled to appear and be heard in person or by counsel.

(7) Upon an application under subsection (5), the court may order notice to be given to any interested person and such person is entitled to appear and be heard in person or by counsel.

120. Subject to the articles, the by-laws or any unanimous shareholder agreement, the directors of a corporation may fix the remuneration of the directors, officers and employees of the corporation.

BIBLIOGRAPHY

Amirault, E. J., and Archer, M. *Canadian Business Law*. Toronto: Methuen Publications, 1976.

Bacon, Jeremy. *Corporate Directorship Practices: Compensation 1975*. New York: The Conference Board, Inc., 1975.

_____. *Corporate Directorship Practices: Membership and Committees of the Board*. New York: The Conference Board, Inc., 1973.

Bacon, Jeremy and Brown, James K. *The Board of Directors: Perspectives and Practices in Nine Countries*. New York: The Conference Board, Inc., 1977.

_____. *Corporate Directorship Practices: Role, Selection and Legal Status of the Board*. New York: The Conference Board, Inc., 1975.

_____. *The Board of Directors: New Challenges, New Directions*. New York: The Conference Board, Inc., 1972.

Baillie, James C. "Steps to Be Taken by Reporting Issuers to Comply with the Securities Act 1978." Paper given at Insight Conference, Toronto, 24 September, 1979.

Barr, Joseph W. "The Role of the Professional Director." *Harvard Business Review*, May-June 1976, pp. 18-19.

"Big Investors on Edge." *The Financial Post*, 24 March, 1979, p. 1.

Bliss, Michael. *A Canadian Millionaire*. Toronto: Macmillan Publishing Company, Inc., 1978.

Brown, Courtney C. *Putting the Corporate Board to Work*. New York: Macmillan Publishing Company, Inc., 1976.

Brown, R. C. "The Legal Responsibilities of a Director." Paper given at *The Financial Post* Conference, Fall 1978.

The Business Quarterly, University of Western Ontario, Summer 1979, p. 23.

Canaero v. O'Malley, [1974] S.C.R. 592.

Canada Business Corporations Act, 1974-75, (Can.), c. 33.

Canada Business Corporation Act, Summary of Highlights. Toronto: Price Waterhouse & Company, 1977.

Carlton Realty Co. Ltd. et al. v. Maple Leaf Mills Ltd. et al. (1979), 22 O.R. (2d) 198.

Craig, W. G. *The Law and Procedure of Meetings in Canada*. Toronto: Ryerson Press, 1966.

Drucker, Peter. *The Concept of the Corporation*. New York: John Day Company, 1972.

Duties and Responsibilities of Board of Directors in Canada. Ottawa: The Conference Board in Canada, 1974.

The Effective Audit Committee. Toronto: Clarkson Gordon & Company, 1977.

Eisenberg, Melvin. *The Structure of the Corporation: A Legal Analysis*. Boston: Little, Brown & Company, 1976.

Etzioni, Amitai. *A Comparative Analysis of Complex Organizations*. New York: The Free Press, 1971.

"Evidence Offers Rare Glimpse of Montreal's Big Business-Political Links" *The Globe and Mail*, 13 June 1979, pp. 1-2.

Evolving Concepts of Prudence: The Changing Responsibilities of the Investment Fiduciary in the Age of ERISA. Charlottesville, VA.: The Financial Analysts Research Foundation, 1976.

"Ex-Boss of Hospital Jailed for 6 Months for Taking Bribes." *Toronto Star*, 1 February 1977, p. B2

"Exxon Records in Canadian Trial Point to Artificially High Oil Price." *The New York Times*, 30 September 1979, pp. 1, 46.

"Falconbridge Chief Dodges T.V. Cameras. . . ." *Toronto Star*, 12 April 1979, p. E12.

Fellows, Patrick. *Toronto Star*, 6 June 1979, p. B12.

Ferrari, Leslie Ann. *Canadian Directorship Practices: A Profile*. Ottawa: The Conference Board in Canada, 1977.

The Financial Post 500. Summer 1979.

Finlay, J. Richard. "Are Canadian Firms Putting Profits Before Responsibility?" *Toronto Star*, 21 April 1979, p. C4.

"The Great Inco Layoff Dilemma." *The Financial Post*, 4 November 1978, pp. 40-41.

Heath, Morris. *Age and Retirement of Company Directors*. Ottawa: The Conference Board in Canada, 1973.

———. *Size and Composition of Boards of Directors*. Ottawa: The Conference Board in Canada, 1973.

Hospital Trustees as Governors and Managers. Don Mills: Ontario Hospital Association, 1979.

Iacobucci, Frank: Pilkington, M. L.; and Pritchard J. R. *Canadian Business Corporations*. Agincourt: Canada Law Book, 1977, pp. 226-340.

Imperial Oil Ltd. v. Nova Scotia Light and Power Co. Ltd., [1977] 2 S.C.R. 817.

Jacoby, Neil H. *Corporate Power and Social Responsibility*. New York: Macmillan, 1973.

"Judgment Places Greater Liability on Auditing Firms." *The Globe and Mail*, 6 June 1979, p. B1.

Juran, J. M., and Louden, J. Keith. *The Corporate Director*. New York: American Management Association, Inc., 1966.

Koontz, Harold. *The Board of Directors and Effective Management*. New York: McGraw-Hill Book Company, 1967.

Lear, Robert W. "Compensation for Outside Directors." *Harvard Business Review*, November-December 1979, p. 18.

Lewis, Stephen. "Crises on the Job: Work, Health, and Collective Bargaining." Paper given at York University symposium—The Prospects for Man—The Quality of Life, 5 June 1979.

Mace, Myles. "The Board and the New CEO." *Harvard Business Review*, March-April 1977, p. 16.

———. *Directors: Myth and Reality*. Boston: Harvard University Graduate School of Business Administration, 1971.

MacArthur, Jack. "There's 60 Billion in Pension Fund Clout." *Toronto Star*, 9 December 1978, p. B7.

McDougall, W. J., ed. *The Effective Director*. London, Ontario: The School of Business Administration, University of Western Ontario, 1966.

———. *Evolving Responsibilities of the Corporate Director*. London, Ontario: The School of Business Administration, University of Western Ontario, 1966.

McGraw-Hill Code of Ethics. New York: McGraw-Hill Company, Inc.

Miller, Judith. "New Prestige for Those in Firing Trade." *The New York Times*, 18 March 1979, p. F3.

"Minority Shareholders Attack Pop Shoppe's Practices." *The Globe and Mail*, 29 June 1979, p. B6.

Mueller, Robert K. *New Directions for Directors*. Lexington, Mass.: Lexington Books, 1978.

———. *The Corporate Director: New Roles, New Responsibilities*. Boston: Cahners Books, 1975.

———. *The Board Life: Realities of Being a Corporate Director*. New York: Amacom, 1974.

Nader, R.; Green, M.; and Seligman, J.; *Taming the Giant Corporation*. New York: W. W. Norton and Company, 1976.

Nader, R., and Green, M. J., eds. *Corporate Power in America*. New York: Grossman Publishers, 1973.

Nason, John W. *Trustees and the Future of Foundations*. New York: Council on Foundations, 1977.

"New Weapon for Bashing Bosses." *Time*, 23 July 1979, p. 35.

Newman, Peter C. *The Canadian Establishment*, Vol. 1. Toronto: McClelland and Stewart, 1975.

"The Not-so-Secret Life of an MPP." *The Financial Post*, 24 March 1979, p. 6.

Ontario Corporation Law Guide Reports, 31 August 1973, p. 5101. "OSC in for Busy Time as New Security Rules Go into Effect." *The Globe and Mail*, 8 September 1979, p. B1.

Perkins, Donald S. "What the CEO and Board Expect of Each Other." *Harvard Business Review*, March-April 1979, p. 26.

Perry, David. "A Taxpayer's Guide to the Business of Government." *The Financial Post 300*, Summer 1978, p. 47.

Peterson, Susan. *Canadian Directorship Practices: A Critical Self-Examination.* Ottawa: The Conference Board in Canada, 1977.

A Plan for 1978-1983. Toronto: Ontario Mental Health Foundation, 1977.

Powell-Smith, Vincent. *The Law and Practice Relating to Company Directors.* London: Butterworths, 1969.

"Protection for Minority Shareholders." *The Financial Post*, 16 April 1977, p. 4.

Report of the Royal Commission on Corporate Concentration. Ottawa: Ministry of Supply and Service Canada, March 1978.

The Royal Commission on Financial Management and Accountability. Ottawa: Ministry of Supply and Services Canada, 1979.

"Shareholder Assails Talcorp Plan. . . ." *The Globe and Mail*, 30 March 1979, p. B8.

"Shareholders Fight Merger. . . ." *The Financial Post*, 21 July 1979, p. 24.

Smith, R. A. *Corporations in Crisis.* New York: Doubleday and Company, 1966.

Stevens, Geoffrey. "A Success Story, but. . . ." *The Globe and Mail*, 4 February 1977, p. 6.

Stone, Christopher D. "Controlling Corporate Misconduct." *The McKinsey Quarterly*, Winter 1978, p. 68.

———. *Where the Law Ends: The Social Control of Corporate Behavior.* New York: Harper & Row Publishers, 1975.

"The Students Name Names." *The Financial Post*, 27 October 1979. p. 6.

Studies as to the Continuing Significance of Equities in the Canadian Market. Toronto Stock Exchange, September 1976.

Sunnybrook Hospital Act of Incorporation and By-Laws. Toronto, 1978.

"Takeovers." *The Financial Post*, 31 March 1979, p. 1.

Thackray, James C. "Regulation, Profit and the Public Interest." Speech given at the 67th Annual Meeting of the Ontario Chamber of Commerce, Ottawa, 8 May 1979.

"The Top Dozen Salaries." *The Financial Post*, 9 June 1979, p. 1.

Trebing, H. M., ed. *The Corporation in the American Economy.* Chicago: Quadrangle Books, 1970.

"UAW is Dead Serious About Place on Boards." *The Globe and Mail*, 13 August 1979, p. B6.

van Eyck, Robert. *Compensation of Boards of Directors.* Ottawa: The Conference Board in Canada, 1974.

Vance, Stanley. "New Dimensions for Boards of Directors." *Conference Board Record*, November 1971.

Wainberg, J. M., and Wainberg, M. I. *Duties and Responsibilities of Directors in Canada.* 3rd ed. Don Mills: CCH Canadian Limited, 1975.

Watson, Ian, and Wong, Kenneth. *Canadian Directorship Practices: Compensation 1976.* Ottawa: Conference Board in Canada, 1976.

"The Weston Empire." *The Financial Post*, 7 April 1979, p. 2.

White, Terrence H. *Power or Pawns: Boards of Directors in Canadian Corporations.* Don Mills: CCH Canadian Limited, 1978.

"Worker-director Plan Strains West Germany's Industrial Peace." *The Financial Post*, 8 September 1979, p. 14.

INDEX

Adams Committee, 55
Air Canada, 13
Albury, 43
Allied Chemicals, 69
Amalgamated Clothing and Textile
  Workers, 85-86
Annual Report, 66
Argus Corporation, 53
Arthur D. Little, Inc., 62
Associate British Foods Limited, 81
Atomic Energy of Canada Limited, 50
Auditor
  ambiguity in role of, 99
  new role of, 54-55, 92, 100-101
  selection and dismissal of, 61, 64, 71,
    100
Authority
  of board, 21-24, 50, 56, 64, 71, 76,
    83-84, 99-100, 110, 118
  delegation of, 17, 21-22, 51, 59-60
  of management, 21, 23-24, 38, 50, 56,
    71, 75, 99-100
Avon Products, 85

Baillie, James, 31, 109
Bank Act, 20
BarChris, 37-39
Beck, Professor Stanley, 23, 26
Bell Canada, 5, 71
Benchley, Robert, 1
Board of Directors
  and accountability, 2-4, 9, 22-24,
    33-36, 93, 103, 110
  and allocation of power between
    parent and subsidiary, 75-81, 83,
    107-108
  ambiguity in role of, 15, 35, 42,
    98-99, 103, 107-109
  changes required in role of, 90, 94,
    96-98, 100, 102, 107-113, 119-120
  and compensation, 15, 64, 104,
    115-116
  composition of, 8-9, 95-97, 103-104,
    113-115

criticisms of, 2-3, 7, 9, 44
duties of, 8-9, 14, 20-21, 24, 29-31,
    33-39, 41, 44, 47-69, 75-84, 86, 89,
    95-96, 99-103, 107-111
effectiveness of, 4-5, 7-8, 53, 68-69,
    87-89, 91-94, 107-108, 111-112,
    114-118
election of members, 1-2, 21, 28, 61,
    64-65, 73-74, 79, 98
ethos of, 88
fiduciary duties, 24-27, 34-36, 40-41,
    84
financial planning and control, 52-55,
    61-62, 67, 92, 100
foreign representation on, 29
legal liabilities of, 6-7, 22-23, 29-31,
    33, 38-39, 41, 76-77, 95, 101
and management, 8, 38, 47, 53, 71,
    81, 83, 89, 95, 107, 111
minority representation on, 3, 60, 65,
    115
power structure of, 87-88
termination of membership on, 19,
    27, 64-65, 80
traditional role of, 8, 67, 89, 94, 107,
    119
worker representation on, 2-3,
    113-114
Boards, governing
  of colleges and universities, 5, 52, 67,
    86, 112-113
  of hospitals, 62, 91, 112
Brascan, 28, 33
British Columbia Companies Act, 19
Bronfmans, 81
Brown, Courtney, 62, 112
Brown, Jr., R. Manning, 86
Bullock Report (Britain), 3
By-laws, 23, 51, 59-61, 64-66, 99, 110

Canada Business Corporations Act, 14,
    19-24, 26-30, 44, 48, 60-61, 64, 76, 99,
    114

143